Belltown Paradise

THE BELLTOWN P-PATCH

COTTAGE PARK

GROWING VINE STREET

BUSTER SIMPSON

EDITORS
Brett Bloom
Ava Bromberg

WHITEWALLS EDITOR
Anthony Elms

DESIGN
Department of Graphic Sciences

Belltown Paradise/Making Their Own Plans (ISBN 0-945323-05-0) was compiled by
Brett Bloom and Ava Bromberg who work together as In the Field.
www.inthefield.info

Published by WhiteWalls, Inc., a not-for-profit corporation,
P.O. Box 8204, Chicago, Illinois 60680

Funding for the production and publication of this book comes from
The City of Seattle's Office of Art and Cultural Affairs
and Seattle City Light % for Art Funds.

Contributions and gifts to WhiteWalls, Inc., are tax-deductible to the extent allowed by law.
This publication is supported in part by grants from the Illinois Arts Council,
a state agency; by a CityArts grant from the City of Chicago Department
of Cultural Affairs; and by our friends and subscribers. WhiteWalls, Inc., is a member
of the Illinois Arts Alliance and the National Association of Artists Organizations.

IMAGES ON COVER
top: *Shared Clothesline: Banners of Human Reoccupation*, by Buster Simpson
bottom: Summer flowers in the Belltown P-Patch. Photo, Myke Woodwell

Table of Contents

Forward

I moved to Belltown from the Pike Place Market in 1996. I remember thinking that Belltown was rather far from the social scene of downtown Seattle, far enough to be filled with semi-industrial buildings and dilapidated old structures. Now it is downtown.

There were a few bright spots in the area, including good people, good food, and the salt and seaweed smell at low tide. I could see the P-Patch from my windows. I got a little plot right away and commenced planting. At that time, the gardening was more about talking to the other folks who showed up to water and weed, commiserating and cheerleading as the topic of conversation demanded. Our garden activities entailed picking up garbage more than determining which variety of asparagus would do best in urban conditions. But there was always new growth, new blooms, and good smells to more than reward a walk to the P-Patch. I got to know the other gardeners. I was grateful for all their efforts and am amazed at all that has been accomplished.

The Seattle Arts Commission (now the Office of Arts and Cultural Affairs for the City of Seattle) was piloting a program called ArtsUp. The idea was to have an artist engage with a community group on a project with the intent of bettering life in the city. My name was put forward as the community liaison for a project with the P-Patch. Given how many new projects started every spring in the P-Patch, it seemed reasonable to think we could identify some endeavor that could benefit from the eye of an artist. Glenn MacGilvra, Artis the Spoonman, and I went to the offices of SAC. We reviewed portfolios of artists selected for the pilot program, made a preliminary choice, and after spending a full day at a "get to know the artists" event hosted by SAC, we selected Brett Bloom, an artist and activist. His work was conceptual, engaging, ephemeral, and strong— just like the P-Patch. I thought he could offer a new perspective on the P-Patch, articulating its value to a larger group beyond the gardeners and the immediate neighbors, and deeply engaging with the many different people who had an individual appreciation or use of the P-Patch.

As a gardener and a close neighbor, I see this book as a chronicle of the determination, conviction, and devotion that is manifest in the P-Patch today. It is testament to an insistent will to make our little corner of Belltown thrive.

Our thanks are due to Brett, for helping us to see the human beauty of the P-Patch and for inspiring us to keep going. The Office of Arts and Cultural Affairs for the City of Seattle warrants acknowledgement, too, especially Lisa Richmond and Kelly Davidson, for sponsoring the ArtsUp project and for their enthusiasm through its circuitous development. And I would like to extend my personal appreciation to Myke Woodwell and Glenn MacGilvra, who, in my mind, are the reason we have the P-Patch and the Cottages.

—Edie Adams

Introduction

This book has taken four years to compile. It is the culmination of many visits, discussions, proposed and rejected projects, and a residency, which all happened in and around a site at the corner of Vine Street and Elliot Avenue in Seattle's Belltown neighborhood.

This site at the corner of Vine and Elliot has a complicated history. It took me a long time to understand what is happening there and its relevance to the greater Belltown area.

The site seems simple enough when you visit; you find beautiful gardens with vegetables and flowers, a city park with three wooden worker's cottages that have been restored and now host residencies for writers, and the beginning of Vine Street's transformation into an environmentally and people-centered green street. What is missing when you visit is direct access to the multiple stories, struggles, volunteer work, meetings, and other long processes that make the place a mini-paradise in one of Seattle's most densely populated neighborhoods.

The gardens are a P-Patch, which means they are city-owned but community run. The P-Patch program is a wonderful city initiative that maintains open urban space for community gardens all over Seattle.

Adjacent to the P-Patch is Cottage Park, which literally grew out of the P-Patch. Three former worker's houses, the last remaining single-family wooden structures in all of downtown Seattle, were neglected and rotting on the privately-owned property next door. Several people instrumental in establishing the P-Patch took on the enormous task of rehabilitating the cottages. The property is now a city park and the cottages house writers-in-residence and a community center.

Growing Vine Street (GVS) is another initiative that came from the energy behind the P-Patch and the determination of nearby residents. The long-term goal behind GVS is to turn Vine Street into a green street—a park that cleans the environment while providing open space for residents. GVS has the potential to eventually close the street to anything but foot traffic.

far left: Mended limb with crutch as splint on street in Belltown, a project by Buster Simpson

Lewis "Buster" Simpson has had an enormous aesthetic impact on these initiatives and on the neighborhood. I repeatedly came across Buster's artwork during my visits to the site and on walks around Belltown. You can find his work on the tops of buildings, integrated into downspouts, temporarily placed on street corners, protecting trees from cars, and in other locations.

Looking at the surrounding buildings and P-Patch from the cottages
Photo, Brett Bloom

A lot of the work Buster has been involved with was ephemeral and only exists in documentation, much of which is included in this book. The amount of work Buster has done in Belltown and the thinking that has accompanied it is stunning. I was surprised that a history of Buster's work in Belltown had never been made. It is important well beyond Belltown and Seattle.

The story of this site is also one of rapid urban change, human displacement, shifting populations, city planning versus local needs, migrant workers, drug addicts, viable artist communities, grunge rock, speculators, dot-com millionaires, homeless men and women, and more.

Through many conversations with The Friends of Belltown P-Patch, gardeners and visitors, it became clear what issues this book should address. There was a desire to make the complicated history of this site visible to the immediate area, greater

Seattle, and beyond. This last concern inspired the second book, attached to this one, which puts the story of this site in dialogue with similar initiatives in other cities.

I would like to thank Glenn MacGilvra, Edie Adams, and Myke Woodwell for putting up with me for the four years it took to finish this project. I would also like to thank Buster Simpson for contributing to this book and for inspiring me, and an entire neighborhood, to think differently about art, ecology, and how they interface with urban realities.

Special thanks go to Ava Bromberg for her tireless hours of editing on both books. The second book would not have been possible without the generous sharing of her independent research.

—Brett Bloom

Belltown P-Patch and Cottage Park

BY GLENN MACGILVRA

Every community garden is the story of a piece of land and a group of people determined to garden it. In the case of the Belltown P-Patch, the land in question is a lot at the corner of Elliott Avenue and Vine Street near downtown Seattle, off to the edge of a neighborhood now known as Belltown. Like many streets and neighborhoods in Seattle it was named after an early pioneer and real estate speculator, in this case William Bell. It is an area of restaurants, condominiums, and small and medium-sized office buildings. The P-Patch is on a small 7200 square foot lot. It sits on a slope between a one-way avenue, Elliott, and an alley.

There is a lot of prehistory, geological upheaval, and Native American history to hurry over. At one time, for example, Elliott Avenue was the shoreline where Native Americans beached their canoes off Elliott Bay. Now the water is a couple of blocks away beyond where the bay was filled in.

I did not get involved with the Belltown P-Patch until June 21, 1995 when I wandered down for the first time to see this cool new community garden I had heard about. I got sucked into blowing up balloons for the opening day celebration. I have been hanging around the place ever since. By then, however, the garden had many years of history behind it.

The story begins more or less in 1910. Seattle was just a few years past the Alaskan Gold Rush and about to enter another economic boom during World War I. Trade at the Seattle docks and nearby was increasing steadily. Five shotgun shacks were built on the corner lot, each 30 by 15 feet with privies in their tiny backyards. A few years later, on the neighboring lot to the south, another six cottages were built, each 20 by 24 feet. These were "modern" cottages with indoor plumbing and "electricity," which consisted of a light bulb hanging from the ceiling.

A real estate speculator and developer named William Hainsworth owned all eleven houses. He marketed them to blue-collar workers making good wages, employed in the shipyards, docks, stores, and nearby fishing boats. A 1920 census showed a range of people and professions living in the area

far left: Myke's Cottage
Photo, Myke Woodwell

including women, children, Croatians, Germans, and Scotts. The cottages remained the same for the next 40 years, as a cluster of small houses for the working class. At some point in the 1930s, the lots were divided into separate little tax lots and sold off to those living in the houses. The houses were passed down to friends and family members.

The cottages when they were new, circa 1916
Photo courtesy of the Hainsworth family

Meanwhile, Belltown changed around them. All the other little wooden houses, as well as most of the tenement houses, were torn down and replaced by apartment buildings, gas stations, commercial buildings, and parking lots. Sometime in the 1960s, all five of the shotgun shacks were torn down. Joe Diamond, owner of Diamond Parking Co., one of the nation's oldest parking lot companies, acquired four of the five lots. Skip Kotkins, owner and manager of Skyway Luggage Company, which had offices nearby, purchased the six-cottage lot next door and tore down three.

That situation, three little houses on one lot next to an empty lot on the corner, stayed the same for the next 25-30 years. During this time Joe Diamond refused to sell to Skip. The houses were rented out by Skyway to various people and the empty lot next door was left to grass, brush, trash, and casual camping.

The story of the people behind the P-Patch can be traced to 1981. At that time, Katherine Shedd moved into one of the cottages. She helped run a vegetable stand at the Pike Place Market about five blocks away. Though not an artist herself, she had friends who were; Buster Simpson and Carl Smool lived across

Vine Street in an old yellow wooden tenement building, one of the few left downtown. Carl, Katherine, and Buster began gardening the backyard of the three cottages, putting in vegetables, paths, and decoration.

Around 1985 or 1986, Katherine moved to Vashon Island and traded her lease to Myke Woodwell for his used mountain bike. The rent at the time was $95 a month.

Myke is a journeyman carpenter, currently an engineer for a truck company. He is a hippie, an inventor (a stair climbing wheelchair), a historian, a photographer, a romantic, mildly pigheaded, but always cheerful. He set about improving his cottage, adding a covered porch, a shed, removing interior walls, and continuing to garden in his backyard. He also acquired a VW Beetle that had rolled over a few times when part of Elliott Avenue caved in during a utilities accident. He cut off the top, put on roll bars, and raced his "Baja Bug" around and around the empty lot next door. As he noted later, it kept the transients out. After every Christmas, he and his friends would take their Christmas

trees out to the lot and set them on fire. It was a corner of downtown Seattle strangely neglected by the authorities.

In 1988, Wilbur "Wilds" Hathaway, another interesting guy who lived in the neighborhood, had the idea of starting a community garden in Belltown. His notion was to put it on an empty

Glenn MacGilvra standing in front of the boarded up cottages
Photo, Myke Woodwell

lot that slopes down from Elliott Avenue to the waterfront, where remnants of an old apple orchard could still be found. It is now the site of a Port of Seattle office building. Wilbur put an ad in the local newspaper, The Denny Dispatch. Wilbur, Myke, Wendy Oberlin, Shirley Schire, and Nancy Allen, the latter a coordinator of the City's P-Patch Program, gathered in a nearby costume shop run by Wendy. After kicking around Wilbur's idea for a while, Myke suggested they cross the street and take a look at the vacant lot next to his house. The five gathered there and found empty mattresses, forty-ouncers, cardboard, and blackberries. They looked upon the land and thought it good.

The five started a round of community gatherings, meetings, and wrote letters to local officials. The preeminent civic institution in the Regrade (its name at the time, Belltown being a later, retro notion) was the Crime Prevention Council run by Jan Drago (now a city council member). The Crime Prevention Council approved of the plan for a P-Patch. Politicians like Norm Rice (former mayor), Ron Sims (now county executive), and Larry Phillips (county council member) also wrote letters of support. An informal group, the Friends of the Belltown P-Patch, was formed.

The problem was not getting support. The problem was money. The empty corner lot was divided between Joe Diamond and Skyway Luggage Co., and neither was known to give away land. The Seattle Parks Department had no money to buy land. Neither did the city's P-Patch program, which relied on donations of land and unused city-owned properties for its community gardens.

Luckily, in 1989, King County passed an Open Space Bond, gathering funds for the purchase of open space in a fast growing region. The competition was stiff. In addition to properties planned for purchase in the bond, there was enough money to acquire another twelve parks countywide, based on citizen nominations. Over 133 properties were nominated.

The Friends of the Belltown P-Patch, a merry band of citizen activists, lobbied the Citizen's Parks Oversight Committee by baking them cookies, handing out fresh vegetables, and chalking flowers on the sidewalk in front of the meeting room. Wendy Oberlin, the costume designer, made trees, squash, gnomes, and hags who haunted the nomination meetings. The Friends of the Belltown P-Patch started making all the newspapers and soon became notorious.

Volunteers crowded the meetings to speak and argue. It was acknowledged that the amount of money needed to purchase the land was awfully big considering the small size of the lot. One member of the committee noted that for the same price, the county could get ten acres of suburban woods. On the other hand, there was not a lot of open space in Belltown; downtown Seattle was slated for higher density. Green space would make the area attractive, and the neighborhood really wanted it.

The property, or at least Joe Diamond's four-fifths, was purchased in 1993 at a cost of around $450,000. A nearby developer gave the Friends $30,000 in exchange for being allowed to limit access to an alley. The city provided $45,000 in matching funds from the Department of Neighborhoods. The land was cleared, a concrete bulkhead built against Elliott Avenue, and hundreds of cubic feet of new topsoil brought in. There was

Mosaic mural on concrete bulkhead
Photo, Myke Woodwell

wrangling over design and fierce arguments regarding paths, the gist of which I could never quite follow when hearing of them later. After two years and a lot of very hard work, much of it managed by Myke—work harder than lobbying, harder than chalking sidewalks, harder than writing letters or histories—the garden was built.

This takes us to 1995. Lovely opening day, balloons and costumes galore, music by the Black Cat Orchestra, food from somewhere, speeches by dignitaries, tours provided by local transvestites, happiness all around. Presiding was another key figure, Eulah Sheffield. She had, at some point, married Myke and moved into his cottage. She was a painter and web designer who could calm dissension, invite participation, facilitate consensus, and still maintain a sense of humor. She had led the Friends for a number of years. For opening day, she wore a blue fairy costume provided by Wendy and led a costumed band around Belltown, from restaurant to restaurant, inviting people to come see the garden.

So then what? What do you do with success? For the next years, the P-Patch peacefully flourished. Wilbur had a plot with teepees and crystals. Others had garden statuary. On the concrete bulkhead a talented artist put in several large mosaic murals of fish, bugs, bees, and sunflowers covering most of the surface. Myke continued to make improvements here and there, and hosted parties in the backyard of his cottage. I came by on occasion and, in collaboration with local architect Carolyn Geise, incited interest in persuading the city to make Vine Street into a "green street," ripping out the pavement and installing an orchard. That idea continues, in various designs, as Growing Vine Street.

Fence, gate, and
solar-powered fountain
Photo, Myke Woodwell

• • •

An observer, however, would note a peculiarity, and a perceptive observer, a growing peril. The peculiar thing was, as noted, the P-Patch covered four-fifths of the lot. It was not a contiguous four-fifths. There was a strip owned near the alley, and also three strips from Elliott Avenue heading uphill. In between was 20 feet by 60 feet covered by grass and owned by Skip Kotkins. How that one lot got into Skip's hands and the rest into Joe Diamond's is lost to history. One popular account holds the seller had a sense of humor. Skip did not sell in 1993. The consequence was a divided garden, leaving the 20-foot strip of P-Patch next to the alley as an orphan. Transients and drinkers enjoyed hanging out in the grassy strip between, and technically, the gardeners had no right to oust them.

One might assume that eventually Skip would sell. What could he do with a single 20-foot strip? Unfortunately, there was the less obvious peril: Seattle's economic boom.

Jeff Bezos, the founder of Amazon, lived a few blocks away. Bill, the Dark Lord of Redmond, made money for himself and for many, many others at Microsoft. All around Belltown, tall condominiums sprang up to house rich people and the moderately prosperous people who worked for them. To the south of the Belltown P-Patch were the lots owned by Skyway Luggage Co., which held a small old storage building, a gravel parking lot, and the three remaining cottages. Skyway Luggage Company was not a real estate developer and purchased the property years before for expansion of its own business. They moved the factories south and overseas instead, and it made sense to sell the property while the good times were rolling. The zoning on the lots allowed a residential building 120 feet high, quite high enough to shade the Belltown P-Patch at nearly all times of the day.

The first move came from Skyway. They offered to sell, or even give away the missing strip if, in return, the Friends of the Belltown P-Patch agreed not to object to building plans on the remaining part of the block. The proposal became known as the "shadow easement." Although the offer gained support from some city council members, the Friends quickly rejected it.

A year or two later, it became clear that Skyway Luggage decided to sell anyway. They hired a property sale negotiator, put their old factory site up for sale, and gave Myke and Jerry the Drummer (a quiet sort who lived without a stir in another one of the cottages) their notice. The last party Myke held in his cottage was in December 1997.

• • •

Sleeping in the P-Patch
Photo, Myke Woodwell

The cottages were boarded up. Gardeners kept gardening the backyard for a while, but it soon mostly went to seed. Transients slept on the porch, broke into the cottages and quickly trashed them. The sleepers and the drunks started to be seriously oppressive to the gardeners next door.

The Friends rallied to stop the potential threat of a tall building. Various proposals were kicked around and the city lobbied heavily to change regulations to lower the height limits, or put in development restrictions so that any new building would not shade the garden. After a large meeting of activists and city officials, the city went away and came back with a simpler idea: buy the cottage lot and make it a park. The price would be more than $900,000.

That the city would be willing to do something like this is a testament to the imagination and audacity of Seattle city officials (particular appreciation to Council Member Jan Drago, the office of Mayor Paul Schell and Parks Official Don Harris), the pressure of the community, and the fact that the good times were rolling for the city too.

The purchase was completed by 2000. The gardeners quickly incorporated the "missing strip" into the garden. The fate of the cottage property was less clear. The city and parks officials who engineered the purchase had in mind a piece of open space, emphasis on the word "open." Leaving the three cottages on the property was a maintenance problem and inconsistent with park principles. Although the city agreed to let a community process come up with a design for the space, the city officials who stuck their necks out to get the money for us and negotiated the purchase had all assumed that the cottages would be torn down. Among other things, part of the purchase price had come from general revenue (amazing in itself). They hoped to repay the general fund with money from an annually available open space fund. That fund would not be available if there were still structures on the property.

What followed was one of those long Seattle processes. Over the course of the next 18 months, the community would consistently deadlock over the question of whether to keep the cottages, how many, and how it could be done. A strong minority agreed with the city that those semi-historic old little houses should be bulldozed and a sweet little park built in its place. A majority, including Myke and myself, thought that a park without people living in it would simply attract transients and trash. This new park, we thought, would become like the empty lot that the P-Patch had been once. Expanding the P-Patch to include the cottage lot was off the table based on the feeling in the parks department and city council that P-Patches were not really public use. Myke, others, and I are fond of old buildings, and thought it a good idea, if possible, to keep the last little wooden houses left in downtown Seattle.

For a year or so, neither side was able to make their views stick. Some of the city officials felt betrayed; they had bought this property for a bunch of ingrates who would not accept that it was not possible to keep the houses. On the other hand, and I am lucky to live in a city like this, those officials were not of a mind to metaphorically steamroll the opposition, terminate the planning, and literally bulldoze the houses. They had a certain respect for community feeling. And, it was never quite clear, legally, that the city had to repay the general fund or was required to tear the cottages down.

There was one fairly tense meeting in the basement of city hall where an official from the mayor's office openly accused me of lying to the community that the cottages could be saved, and then walked out. But then things calmed down. There was one more community meeting to see what people really thought. Myke and I were careful to pack the meeting with supporters.

The cotteges
before renovation
Photo, Myke Woodwell

There was a nice speech from the head of Historic Seattle, a local preservationist nonprofit. The city finally agreed to keep the three cottages in place, allow some to be used as residences, and continue to work towards figuring out what to do with the others. Shortly afterwards, for purposes of insurance, Myke and I persuaded the city Landmarks Committee to give the cottages landmark status making it much more difficult to tear them down.

After this, there was still more struggle to raise the money needed to renovate the cottages, sadly trashed and abused in the three years they were unoccupied, to make them habitable, manage the construction, and work out the landscape design for the remaining part of the property. One of the more important tasks was to figure out exactly who was going to be in the cottages. We were lucky again, as a Seattle institution, the Richard Hugo House—a literary center named after a local poet—was willing to help. They agreed to make two of the cottages into writer-in-residence spaces.

The fundraising, renovations, and landscaping were stressful and frustrating, as those things tend to be. Myke managed the rehabilitation quite well, working with the parks department and keeping pressure on contractors hired with approximately $350,000 raised from public and private sources, mostly Seattle's Department of Neighborhoods. We are still, actually, in the process, as we have not quite finished off the interior of one cottage, where Myke used to live. A gardener, Rebecca, is

above: The cottages after renovation
Phoro, Myke Woodwell

left: Cottage Park crew

Belltown Inside-out
Community Festival,
August 1997
Photo, Carolyn Geise

working with a friend to make the space serve as café and meeting place for the community. In the meantime, the planting and planning continue. On spring days, like today, the place looks very sweet. We hope for the best. The effort to actually implement the plan has been slow but reasonably steady.

• • •

The people and the neighborhood continue to change. Perhaps it is best summed up by an artist who painted a trashcan with this message: "Move to Belltown. See the Artists. Buy a condo. Kick the artists out." But before I can get too sentimental, I have to remember that if there had not been the change, neither the Belltown P-Patch nor the Cottage Park would have been purchased or built, at least looking as good, or as polished as they do now.

In 1989, the Citizens Oversight Committee, advising regarding the Parks Bond, might not have spent their limited funds in Belltown, except on the assumption the neighborhood would become more densely populated. In 1999, the city made the even tougher decision to buy the cottage lot for the same reason. If a condo had not been blocking an alleyway nearby, the P-Patch would not have received $30,000 to help build the gardens in 1993. Money from another developer, Intracorp, as well as contributions from our longtime neighbor, the Skyway

Luggage Co., helped rehabilitate the cottages. Even though condo owners can be a crabby, selfish, shortsighted lot (I am one, as it happens), for the most part, they wanted this community garden and park. There were more and more of them to make this point.

If the Belltown P-Patch and Cottage Park are a consequence of gentrification, at the very least the gentry do not have to be stuffy. In years past, talented people scraping by in low rent buildings made interesting stuff for public display, ran around in costumes, had solstice celebrations, drove cut-down VWs on empty lots and torched trees on New Year's Day. I only hope that interesting stuff continues to happen here.

Watering the garden
Photo, Myke Woodwell

I was the very first resident at the Cottage Park. I stayed in one of the cottages during July 2003. A lot of people use the gardens. Students from the neighboring art school come over during lunch breaks as do people from local office buildings. Couples pluck flowers for each other and stroll around aimlessly. Gardeners remove weeds and harvest fresh vegetables. Day laborers, unable to get work early in the morning, spend afternoons drinking in the P-Patch or next to the wall on Vine Street. Sometimes people sleep in the garden. Others use it as their toilet or for other illicit activities. It is a very dynamic space, one that is contested on a daily basis. I kept a brief record of goings on in a small part of the garden I came to call "the spot."

The Spot
BY BRETT BLOOM

7/12/03, SATURDAY: There is a particular spot in the Belltown P-Patch that is hidden on most sides. I have the only vantage point through the window in the front door to the cottage I am staying in. The plants around the spot are overgrown and the area is over ten feet above the street level; the entire garden is on a hill that slopes down to Elliot Bay. A large retaining wall holds this end of the garden. The initial group of folks who started the garden built the wall.

I looked through the window, very early in the morning, and saw three people: two women and one man. The man was drinking beer. One woman pulled her pants down to relieve herself. She needed help from the other two to even stand up. It was quite sad and pathetic. I decided to let them be, even though the situation made me really tense. They did not stay for very long.

7/13/03, SUNDAY: I saw one man standing looking at the garden. I wondered what he was doing. He actually looked like he was admiring the flowers. A man got up followed by a woman. She pulled her pants up and wiped dirt and other debris from her backside. They had just had sex. The man standing up watching seems to be the "handler" or pimp of two or three homeless women I have seen in the lot across the street and in the garden. I think I saw this woman having sex with another man during last Saturday's work party. She and her john were across the street barely concealed by a fence, weeds, and a large sheet of cardboard.

I heavily watered the spot in the garden to make it undesirable to use. It has not been getting hot enough here during the day to make all of the water evaporate so things stay pretty damp overnight. I also watered other locations that looked as if they were hidden sleeping or resting spots.

The spot, trampled
Photo, Brett Bloom

One of the gardeners later told me that this was a known trouble spot. Someone had been gardening in the location. She gave up once the destruction of her plants started and had not been back at the garden since. This, I was told, happened frequently.

7/14/03, MONDAY: I went out this morning to water the homeless—actually to use water and my presence as a deterrent to homeless men and women drinking, urinating, defecating, having sex, and killing plants in "the spot." I was surprised to find that no one was there. The garden plot had been "defended" with shards of concrete, large rocks, and a barrier of string and chicken wire attached to wooden stakes. There was a large pile of wet human excrement and pages from one of the local, free newspapers on the path. I used the hose to wash the pile away and to decrease the stench of urine that permeates this area.

A couple of hours later, three men and two women were in this area again. They were drinking and having sex. One of the community members asked them to leave. When I told her that they were there having sex yesterday, she informed them that the police would be called the next time they were there. They slowly left the area. One silent, belligerent, inebriated man slowly picked up beer cans and took his time leaving. He did not hide his contempt for us. The community member who was with me—she is average height and can be loud when she needs to—told me of altercations that have turned violent because she has confronted people. One encounter escalated to this woman hosing down a drunken man who then started to throw rocks at her. A parking lot attendant from across the street intervened before it got too out of hand. She also spoke of a time when she had to kick someone in the groin. I did not get the entire story—next time. This community member leaves me things—I call her the tupperware fairy.

The spot, defended
Photo, Brett Bloom

There are plans to dramatically cut back the rose bushes and other tall plants that give safe haven to these not-so-hidden activities. A work party is planned for this evening. There is a citywide open house at all of the P-Patches.

ADDENDUM: When I first visited the P-Patch back in 2000, it was the first time I had ever encountered defensive urban gardening and plot design, an approach for strategically making your plot, or parts of the garden, difficult to destroy or use to hide illicit activities. My initial response was to recoil from this aggressive gardening. I thought that people were overreacting and making public spaces way too individual and private. It was not until coming and living on site that I got a sense of how regular and routine the disrespect and misuse of the garden was. I have seen someone urinating or looking for a place to urinate every day for the past two weeks. On Friday and Saturday nights, it is male patrons of local bars that use the P-Patch as a toilet.

Public urination is a serious problem that is not being addressed in the P-Patch let alone in the city. No one is taking active steps to deal with this problem with long-term solutions. This problem is not going away. The interim solution is to make it as undesirable as possible to use the garden. There is a need for more public resources—toilets being just a small component. There is a larger denial and exclusion built into the infrastructure of this city, a condition that speaks to how privatized our cities' "public spaces" have become. This is a serious cause for concern.

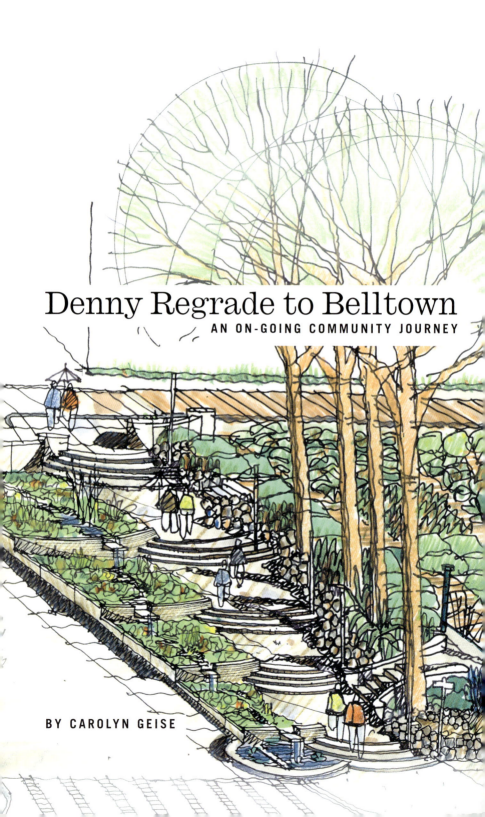

Denny Regrade to Belltown

AN ON-GOING COMMUNITY JOURNEY

BY CAROLYN GEISE

When development finally came to the Regrade area, it took off like a rocket with the economic success of the '90s and the dot-com bubble. There were one or more construction cranes on every block for several years. Many of us in the Regrade looked forward to a more densely populated urban neighborhood, but wondered what we could do to preserve some of the colorful cultural heritage the artists had developed.

Seattle's Comprehensive Plan projected 6,500 additional residents by the year 2014. Their arrival would increase density to 46.3 households per acre, making ours by far the most densely populated neighborhood in Seattle. Change was inevitable, but did it have to be total gentrification? Could the missions, low-income housing, and day-labor centers co-exist with multi-million-dollar condominiums and a fashionable restaurant district? What could the community do to shape this development, to provide breathing room for the new density, keep a touch of nature, and integrate newcomers into the existing fabric of the neighborhood rather than let it be destroyed?

When I joined this community in 1992, the organizers of the fledgling Belltown P-Patch were taking on this challenge. They set about planning a community garden, a public realm where interaction among people of all income levels could take place, tempered with nature, providing opportunities for community building and stewardship. They were creating a vision for a community garden not to just feed the stomach, but to feed the soul. Their garden consisted of art, flowers, and food. It provided a connection to the land desperately needed in this neighborhood of wall-to-wall paving. The Regrade was a location, but the name "Belltown" represented the heart and soul of the community that this valiant group set about saving and expanding. Their motto was a "garden where plants and people flourish." They were on to something and I wanted to help make it happen.

SEEDS OF GROWING VINE STREET

The Frayn Building at 81 Vine Street came on the market at just the time that my family development partnership sold a

far left:
Rendering of the
Cistern Steps
Carlson Architects

building and needed to reinvest. It was a simple three story brick building built as a box factory in 1914 with beautiful large windows grouped into pairs under graceful brick arches. We purchased the building, and when the first stage of renovation was completed in 1994, I moved my office, Geise Architects, into the building. We used the open house as an opportunity to bring our new community together to discuss how we could support the P-Patch plan to expand into Vine Street. The P-Patch had discovered Vine Street was designated as a level 1 green street in the city's 1986 master plan. This classification allowed for pedestrian development into the street and, if desired, the street could even be closed off to motor traffic entirely.

Meanwhile, I was running into problems with the green street requirement for the sidewalk at the 81 Vine Street building. City officials did not agree about exactly what was required when developing along a green street. After spending thousands of dollars on civil engineering and hours going from the building department to engineering, which had control of the street right-of-way, to the city arborist, and around again, I proposed that we leave the sidewalk as is in the first phase of the renovation, since we were just remodelling the existing building. Then, during the second phase addition of seven penthouse units, we would upgrade the sidewalks. We hoped the green street requirements would be clearer by then.

In the meantime Glenn MacGilvra and I began to gather a community group around the issue of how Vine Street could be developed under the green street ordinance, especially beside the P-Patch. Soon Glenn and I were writing the first grant to Seattle's Department of Neighborhoods (DON) for $42,000 to hire a consultant to prepare a concept design for Vine Street based upon bioregional principles and celebrating water. At about 3 a.m., while putting the finishing touches on the application, Glenn came up with "Growing Vine Street," which has served well to title our vision.

EARLY STAGES

Word of the GVS project spread and our small group grew to 15 committed individuals. We attended meetings at least twice a month during 1996 and 1997 to develop preliminary design ideas in preparation for hiring a design team. A primary concern was incorporating ecosystem-based design to bring natural elements back to the city. Inspired by the idealism of the young people in our group, such as aspiring transportation planner Peter Voorhees and architect David Craven, we boldly claimed the full eight blocks of Vine Street as a watershed and defined some ecosystem design guidelines. We invited artist Buster Simpson to these meetings since he was interested in the area and in storm water solutions. He was an inspiring participant in developing the concept of treating and playing with the storm water.

We organized continuous events to raise money and awareness of the project. These events and the many meetings were successful as fundraisers, but more importantly served to unite and define this new community and bring new comers and old timers together around a common goal.

Buster Simpson and Peggy Gaynor planting *Vertical Landscape* at the 81 Vine Street building, 1999
Photo, Paul Joseph Brown, *Seattle Post Intelligencer*

NEIGHBORHOOD PLANNING

Simultaneously, the neighborhood planning process began in Belltown and ran from April 1996 to December 1998. This was a community-driven process that received city funding. Communities hired their own planning consultants and the city provided staff to help keep the process moving. The core values developed by the Denny Regrade Organizing Committee, which included many GVS members, were as follows: The Denny Regrade Neighborhood is an urban community concerned with quality of life and built on social equity, economic viability, environmental stewardship, security, and respect for its cultural and historical traditions.

For much of the process the GVS steering committee served as the Pedestrian Environment Committee for the planning group. The neighborhood planning process was a chance for us to discuss the problems we came up against while developing a street design that was actually a storm water treatment infrastructure. GVS served as a test case for developing well-designed green streets. The Downtown Urban Center Planning Group, a coalition of the five downtown neighborhoods including the Denny Regrade, chose to invest some of their planning money to study the obstacles and solutions to permitting, constructing, and maintaining green streets.

Vertical Landscape downspout on the 81 Vine Street building, 1999
Photo, Carolyn Geise

SELECTING A DESIGN TEAM

By July 1997, the steering committee had defined goals, developed design guidelines, and advertised for a design team. Eight excellent teams responded and we interviewed three. Seventeen members of the committee spent most of a Saturday conducting the interviews and making the decision. Our selection was a multidisciplinary firm organized by Carlson Architects consisting of Don Carlson, architect and urban designer; Greg Waddell, planner; Peggy Gaynor, landscape architect; and Buster Simpson, environmental artist. Aidan Stretch, Sustainable Development Group and Marni Heffron, Heffron Transportation, also provided input. We recognized the challenge of working with such a strong and diverse group, but they fit our vision of being bold, brave, and ecologically minded. We also felt the different talents, ranges of experience, and styles would resonate with the varied constituents in our community. Having Buster on the team was a plus as he was already recognized as the Regrade artist and his work typified the spirit we were trying to capture.

DESIGN CONCEPT DEVELOPMENT

To accommodate the idea of this street as a laboratory for storm water solutions, and to facilitate incremental adoption of the concept by the community, the design team developed a "kit of parts," a guideline for development. This kit is a collection of flexible design elements that create a design framework and provide guidance for long-term development of the green street. There are four core concepts of structure and function: first, the street functions as a one-way driving lane with some back-in parking. Second, we recognize storm water runoff as a resource to be exposed and integrated into the green street philosophy. Third, the greening of the street corridor includes the greening of buildings. Fourth, the greening of Vine Street is an enduring social event providing a venue for creative contributions from the community.

This infrastructure project addressed the issue of regular sewer overflow into Puget Sound. Belltown has a combined sewer and storm water system. Statistics for 2001 show that Seattle had 556 overflow events which dumped 272 million gallons of sewage-tainted water into our natural water systems. Reducing the storm water run off will decrease or eliminate the incidence of overflow.

Our motto was, store the water, enjoy and play with the water, irrigate with the water; do not just send it down a black hole to get rid of it. The project was a winner and people flocked to hear about it and participate.

COMMUNITY OUTREACH & IMPRINTING THE CONCEPT

Development accelerated and new people moved into the community by the hundreds. GVS meetings became updates to the community about how the project was progressing and about new construction in the neighborhood. It seemed that almost every week a new high-rise apartment or condo was being planned. We made a huge map of the neighborhood and pinned up articles about proposed new buildings. As the reality of the growth explosion began to sink in, the need to create a humane pedestrian environment stimulated wider interest in our project.

There were eight major construction projects in the planning stage on the eight-block length of Vine Street during the time we were developing our design concept. Members of the GVS steering committee or design team met with each of the developers to encourage them to take our concept into consideration in their new construction projects. Although none of them incorporated water features, several made supportive landscaping or detail gestures. Once the GVS design concept was approved by the Seattle Design Commission, the new city design department tried to require developers on Vine Street to embrace the GVS concept. Compliance is mostly voluntary, however, since financial incentives are not available.

We presented GVS to community groups, the Design Commission, committees of the City of Seattle Council, and at conferences. The idea began to take hold. GVS became part of the vocabulary of other Seattle communities and was used by city officials as an example of an innovative, community-driven approach to urban storm water solutions.

Detail of the
Beckoning Cistern,
by Buster Simpson
Photo, Carolyn Geise

81 VINE BUILDING
GROWING VINE STREET PROJECTS

With the economy rising in 1997, my development partners decided to proceed with the second phase of adding penthouses on the 81 Vine Building and converting the building to condominiums. This triggered the requirement for sidewalk improvements, but GVS was still working its way through meetings with the city to solve technical issues. My partners generously agreed to wait for GVS, which required

putting off our sidewalk work for two years and posting a bond in order to secure a temporary occupancy permit so we could sell the units.

Bow truss downspout on 81 Vine Street Building
Photo, Carolyn Geise

The 81 Vine Building actually includes three GVS projects. The roof terraces serve as headwaters to GVS with water carried from the roof over the terrace in two graceful bow truss downspouts that feed into a linear galvanized culvert planter with a water distribution system. Water overflowing the planter or collected on the roof is directed through new scuppers in the parapet to channel rainwater to supply GVS. The downspout on the west is a vertical landscape by Buster Simpson, which has four stainless steel planter loops. The eastern downspout drained into the gutter for two years before being hooked up to the *Beckoning Cistern*, also designed by Buster.

The Beckoning Cistern is magical. This huge blue metal cistern is set on a platform canted slightly toward the building with a green metal hand. The index finger reaches over the sidewalk to touch the downspout, which angles out from the building to deposit the roof runoff into the extended finger. When it rains, people come to see water flow from the thumb, into the planter, and then from pool to pool. Buster Simpson and Peggy Gaynor worked with architect Judy Tucker from Geise Architects on this project with special structural consultation by Swenson Say Faget.

OPPORTUNITY TO BUILD THE CISTERN STEPS

We had a developer nearby the P-Patch who was willing to channel their building's roof water across the street to feed the Cistern Steps. John Eskelin and Elisabeth Butler from the DON stepped up and negotiated an Opportunity Grant from the city in the amount of $200,000 so the Cistern Steps portion of GVS could proceed and integrate with the new development. This endorsement of our project gave us additional credibility at a time when we needed positive action to encourage our weary volunteers. We have now broken ground on the Cistern Steps, the second GVS demonstration project.

Breaking ground on the *Cistern Steps*

ENGINEERING DRAWINGS
AND THE PERMITTING PROCESS

Our original design team, with the addition of SvR Design Company, was commissioned by the city to proceed with design refinement and permit documents. SvR were brought in as civil engineers because they grasped the significance of this project and have a strong landscape architecture base. The design team project manager, Gregg Waddell, kept the team moving forward and negotiated through the technical hurdles.

I am used to complex and conflicting codes and regulations, but I had no idea how difficult it would be to build a non-standard design in the street right of way. Although most city officials were inspired by the idea and wanted to help, the official standards and procedures made it difficult. We often came to the point where I would tell the city reviewer to just say "no" if that is what their rules told them to do and I would take it up to the mayor or the council. I knew it was policy that had to change from the top and Mayor Paul Schell was wonderfully supportive. His motto was "neighborhoods that accept density will get amenities" and we were certainly getting density.

In February 1999, Mayor Schell and department heads authorized a technical team to work with our design team and steering committee to solve technical issues before the project could be permitted. We began with a half-day charette at the city, which over 30 staff members attended. By the end of the meeting we identified the issues and the responsible parties to solve them. The city authorized $60,000 to cover staff time and we began regular meetings. Almost a year passed with marginal progress, but thanks to Gregg Waddell a GVS Implementation Guide Book was published in March 2000, which has served as a guide as individual projects on Vine Street are submitted for permit.

KEEPING THE PROJECT ALIVE
AND KEEPING OUR FOCUS

As GVS moved slowly along year by year, we stopped several times to focus energy on the core issues of the Belltown P-Patch. First, the campaign to buy the cottage property to the south and the missing piece in the main patch. Next, the effort to save all three cottages and develop the Cottage Park, and last, the restoration of the cottages. There was some overlap of personnel on all of the projects, but GVS was the spine that connected this marvellous urban oasis to the community and to the waterfront. The P-Patch and Cottage Park were the core projects, so we made every effort to support and not distract from their work to insure proper funding and development. Myke Woodwell and Glenn MacGilvra carried most of the load on those two projects with varying degrees of support and encouragement from the rest of the community.

None of these projects would have happened at all without the DON matching grant program, which director Jim Diers nurtured under the administration of three Seattle Mayors. If we include purchase of the parcels of land and private contributions, over $3,000,000 has been invested into the P-Patch, Cottage Park, and GVS. The GVS portion alone represents an investment of over $800,000. Neither of these figures account for value of the thousands of hours of volunteer labor that have made these projects possible.

My front row seat as both observer and participant in this adventure over the past twelve years has been an extraordinary experience. I am amazed at the number of participants and accomplishments. The strength of the environmental movement and the delayed development in Belltown allowed us to catch a few opportunities before they were lost. The unique combination of artists, residents of all income levels, design professionals, developers, and community-oriented local businesses brought broad-based resources to the project.

GVS opened the way for flexibility in green street design. We discovered that there was no process for permitting a comprehensive green street, no way to pay for it other than on a parcel-by-parcel basis, and no system for handling maintenance. These hurdles have been met and the doors are now open for new projects. By introducing a radical design far outside the standard development guidelines for city streets, we cleared the way for other proposals from neighborhood and city departments.

Although the process of resolving technical and permitting issues seemed frustrating and arduous at the time, as I

Potlach meeting in
the P-Patch
Photo, Carolyn Geise

look back, I see extraordinary support for this project within the
city. Many officials, especially from DON, took big risks in supporting us. The two major demonstration projects, Beckoning
Cistern and Cistern Steps, would not have been possible
without their support.

Projects like the Belltown P-Patch, Cottage Park, and GVS
are a testament to the survival of the original Belltown spunk
and sparkle. The stage is set for the full GVS vision to unfold. I
hope this story gives a sense of the energy of these combined
projects, an energy that could not be dampened, no matter what
obstacles appeared.

Perpendicular & Parallel Streetscape Stories

BY BUSTER SIMPSON

Downtown Seattle, Pike Place Market and the Belltown neighborhood served as locations for all of my studios from 1974 through 1987. Most were on a month-to-month basis, which had its economic advantages, but logistical shortcomings necessitating a move about every two years. Almost all the studio locations were on First Avenue or fronted Post Alley which runs parallel to the west of First Avenue. These two historic spines were my desire lines and became my public laboratories: the front door onto First Avenue, and its back door counterpart, Post Alley. The Avenue, with its veneer façade, window dressing, and commerce, was countered by the alleyway's transparency, ad hoc retrofits, and utility. Perpendicular to and intersecting these two parallel conveyances is Vine Street.

My last studio and residence in Belltown was located on Western Avenue. An adjacent vacant lot on Vine Street became a shared garden. This garden was the precursor to what eventually became the Belltown P-Patch. The P-Patch precipitated an ongoing project called Growing Vine Street, begun in 1996.

The neighborhood population has more than doubled since 1974 and with this increase came the growing pains characteristic of a community redefining itself.

LEARNING FROM THE NEIGHBORHOOD

Post Alley served as my studio entrance at five different locations and became the basis of some early projects. In 1978, when I was living and working in a space on Post Alley below a fixed income residence, a new condominium had just been completed across the alley, creating a potential economic mix that makes cities interesting. I conceived and installed a working series of clotheslines between these two buildings connecting four floors and their inhabitants with their neighbors across the alley: the fixed income renters with the new condominium owners. I called this piece *Shared Clothesline: Banners of Human Reoccupation*. The installation proclaimed sustainability as well as social issues, as a dramatic agit prop of utility—what I later called "poetic

far left:
Shared Clothesline: Banners of Human Reoccupation,
Solar Day 1978

utility." The clothesline was introduced on Solar Day in 1978 with an entire load of wash dyed yellow. This functional urban amenity served as an alternative to electric dryers as well as a response to the proliferation of the decorative "identity package" banners marketing a lifestyle rather than providing an authentic urban experience. Furthermore, many of the new condominiums had covenants against hanging clothes out to dry on individual balconies, which was considered "unsightly." The clotheslines could be used by neighbors on either side of the alley to dry clothing, or, I mused, a cup of sugar could traverse the gap. When the line was bare and wind gusted through the alley, the line functioned as an Aeolian harp providing acoustical resonance.

2001 First Avenue studio during demolition, 1978

Most residents and pedestrians walking through Post Alley appreciated the clothesline. One gentleman from the fixed income residence took offense to what he considered a reminder of his unpleasant past of being forced to hang his laundry out to dry. Eventually, he cut down all the lines. I learned from this the humility of working in shared space, and the patience such work requires. The piece remains a memory awaiting a paradigm shift.

FIRST AVENUE STREETSCAPE PROJECT

Artists residing in the Belltown neighborhood initiated the First Avenue streetscape project in 1978. What ultimately developed has become an ongoing innovative approach to streetscape design. Artists agreed to assist the Denny Regrade Community Council in conceptualizing and implementing projects on an eleven-block section of First Avenue centered north of the downtown Seattle core in the midst of Belltown. The project was treated as a work in process, a laboratory for untried approaches and solutions to urban design. Considering that there was little or no budget, this was realistic. The aesthetic was intentionally ad hoc and looked as though it had simply happened rather than been designed. This was a rejection to the commonly applied identity packages, branding, and way-finding clichés typical of a top-down design approach. We never invoiced for our "final billing" in 1984, so, technically, this project is still on the books.

The first concern of the community was to find something to sit on while waiting at the bus stops. There was interest in creating shade and greenery as well. The solution needed to be cost-effective and able to withstand the rigors of urban wear and erosion. The city engineering departments had their concerns about anything unique and not easily replicable. Their

Sandstone ready-mades at bus stop on First Avenue at Wall prior to re-siting the bus stop at Cedar Street, c 1984

prime concern, as was ours, was that we did not create a harmful public liability.

Working with the city was an ongoing waltz to push their envelope while respecting their issues. We called the street project a "laboratory" as a design strategy, and often used the term "temporary prototypes" as a non-threatening rationale to achieve an innovative street amenity. These streetscape projects prompted a discussion among artists, community, and the city that ultimately led to a consensus. The relationship has provided an open-ended unofficial channel for aesthetic discourse as First Avenue in Belltown continues to be developed.

The changing demographic since 1978 has tested the laboratory approach as the streetscape has become more populated. The single-resident occupancy hotels built in the late 1800s and early 1900s were once the dominant housing stock in the neighborhood. In the 1980s they were demolished and replaced with condominiums and rental units. Developers, in an attempt to attract new residents, often based the aesthetics of a project on marketing trends, which were uninformed about neighborhood context and did not address social and sustainability issues. When

above: Key stones sited on First Avenue and Broad Street (site of the first of three relocations)

right: Sandstone key stones removed from the state capital and in storage at Wilkeson Sandstone Quarry before siting

new developers attempted to assert their design on our pre-existing streetscape they were instructed that both city and federal art funding protected the various amenities such as trees, artifacts, and benches. This provided leverage to negotiate for something better, if the developers were willing to invest in an idea bigger than their own frontage. By and large developers agreed to collaborate. To this day, the street design intends to integrate new developments and their needs with those of the greater community and its eleven-block episodic journey along First Avenue. The First Avenue approach strives to be dynamic, encouraging the ongoing layering of meanings. Discovering an anomaly from the past juxtaposed with the present is the essence of the urban; a sophisticated place allows us to read through the layers ultimately becoming our legacy.

BUS SHELTERS

Providing a place to rest and wait along the First Avenue bus stops initiated a new street friendly social gathering place. The city budgeted enough money for the least expensive off-the-shelf bench solution. We chose to take that budget and select what we rationalized as "ready-mades"—sandstone remnants from the Wilkeson Sandstone Quarry in Wilkeson, Washington. This quarry operated since 1886 supplying dimensional stone to some of the region's significant architecture. The quarry had just declared bankruptcy and we were one of the first to salvage relics such as the original keystones from the state's capital building, which were replaced after the 1949 earthquake.

The stone benches were sited at each of the nine bus stops and augmented with a grove of purple plum trees that we planted to provide cover and a color code visible down the length of the street. Cluster planting lessened heat stress on the city street trees. The color-coded bus locations had their drawbacks when Metro moved or consolidated a few of its bus stop locations leaving the purple plums. Relocating the benches required a Sunday morning mobilization and consultation with the transit planners. A working relationship developed between the different governmental agencies involved in these streetscape decisions and a consensus was reached.

As the demographic changed in the 1990s and the new residents and merchants were not yet acclimated to the neighborhood, benches began to be perceived as magnets for "undesirables." There were city council hearings and community meetings, but the most effective approach to education was on-site dramatization of the issue. One such example was the "butt guard," a device that temporarily rendered the bench unusable while postings described the reason why the device had been installed. The benches are now an accepted part of the streetscape.

Community planting of Gary oak

THE URBAN ARBORETUM

The Urban Arboretum provided the First Avenue streetscape laboratory an opportunity to expand the city's acceptable palette of street tree choices. Aside from issues of invasive root structures, short-lived and brittle trees, the city's palette excluded many indigenous varieties for no apparent reason. America's urban street trees are more and more a monoculture of obedient vertical hybrids that keep out of our way and do not make a mess. This project was a refreshing opportunity to question that restrictive attitude. We were interested in creating a diverse urban arboretum to monitor the trees' ability to grow.

One of the first events was an Arbor Day interventionist planting of two hundred seedlings. The seedlings were given away with instructions on how and where they were to be planted. "No man's lands" and formal corporate landscapes, such as the large office towers being built on 4th Avenue with suburban landscaping, were among the suggested locations for planting.

One of the first trees to be introduced, or re-introduced, was the cedar tree. Because of our efforts, cedars are now included in other downtown streetscape designs. The laboratory was working. Other unique specimens included gingko, flowering dogwood, vine maple, and magnolia, interspersed with other trees, creating a unique rhythm of tree types and spacing. Another innovation was that the trees were not planted in a straight line. In addition to grove clustering at bus stops, we staggered trees between property line and curb to provide a weave to the pedestrian's walk. The city's only criterion in developing this design was to maintain a 4-foot wide, unobstructed pathway along the weave for wheelchair accessibility.

My studio at 2001 First Avenue accommodated a sixty-year-old Queen Anne fruiting cherry tree, and was surrounded by turn-of-the-century architecture. After an unsuccessful battle by housing and tree advocates, who equated displacement of people with the destruction of this tree, in 1979 this historic cherry tree became the first of the "witnesses" removed to make way for one of the first condominium developments along First Avenue. As a result of the attention this issue brought to the community, it was pointed out that preservation should include not only architecture, but also living things. Shortly after this battle, a fruiting cherry tree, which had been a survivor of pre-renovation of the Pike Place Public

Front Page of the Belltown Rag featuring the removed Queen Anne cherry tree, December 1979

Market, was threatened by new development. After three hearings in the mid-1980s, where the developer paraded in experts to testify that the tree would not survive the new development, the historic commission issued a mandate to the developer to accommodate the tree with the new construction. The tree thrives to this day as a living relic.

above: Location of the fruiting cherry tree with text on fence and dancing figure tree guards

far right, top: Salvaging the Gary oak from the city landscape dump

far right, bottom: Gary oak re-sited on First Avenue

On First Avenue, adjacent to the site of the Queen Ann's demise, a new fruiting cherry was planted as a replacement. The fence next to the new planting was painted with text, which provides passing pedestrians with a historical account of the cherry tree succession, and a pedestrian treatise explaining the urban design forces in play. Even though birds generally consume the cherries before they constitute a liability, allowing fruiting cherry trees as street trees is a subtle victory. These are the only fruiting street trees downtown. The historical precident overrode the developer's desire to plant a flowering, ornamental cherry tree. The tree guard we placed around the fruiting cherry was fashioned from branches gleaned from the fallen Queen Anne. The installation suggested three dancing figures with faces consisting of plates, which also served as bird feeders. There was a heated discussion with the developer about the aesthetic merits of this piece and its placement in front of his corporate building. His hired handyman removed and destroyed the tree-guard under the cover of darkness.

When possible, the community was involved with the street tree planting to foster stewardship. On one occasion, some city officials believed the selected type of tree, an oak, would not survive the urban environment. Not long after the community planting we noticed that the tree was removed professionally, which indicated to us that it was the work of the city rather than vandalism. We asked, "Why?" They replied, "It was dead." We knew it was alive because we had just checked the tree. We went to the city landscape dump and found, retrieved, and replanted the oak. Fortunately the root ball was intact although its trunk had been cut in half. The tree was replanted and it sprouted new shoots. A cage was installed around it. An ax head was buried in the "stump" of the trunk and the project documented. The oak thrived and the city realized the seriousness of our intent. Four years later, when a new development again threatened the tree, the construction workers worked around it and protected the tree until someone from the city ordered it removed. We lost this opportunity for yet another chapter in the saga of this particular tree. In 2002, two Gary oaks were planted as part of a condominium streetscape agreement supporting the urban arboretum concept. The struggle of the oak was now secure in the institutional memory. Its planting went unopposed.

The informal day-to-day monitoring of clandestine projects was giving way, due to the rapid development of the neighborhood, to the need for a formal process.

TREE GUARDS

In the late 1970s, First Avenue was in transition. Dotted along the Avenue were old sailor bars, such as the "Fore and Aft," which offered a 6 a.m. happy hour. As patrons left the bar and navigated the street, these young trees offered their tender limbs to the passing intoxicated pedestrians needing to stabilize their

above left: Gary oak one year later

above right: *Tree Guard* stake and watering pipe

passage, subsequently deforming the branches. The city considered these trees damaged and expendable and was prepared to remove them. We argued that these deformed trees would grow to represent a living testimony to this time in Seattle's transitional history. We called this benign act "Urban Bonsai." We saw a parallel between these urban forces and those found at timberline where the trees physically express the environmental conditions of the location.

To brace the damaged or broken limbs, we bound them with cloth using a crutch as a splint. Occasionally we noticed a crutch had mysteriously disappeared. We found out that some people who needed a crutch for their own assistance would remove it from the tree unaware of its intended function.

Eventually, with repeated reinstallations, the poetic utility of the crutch mending the limb was understood.

Additional approaches to tree guards were implemented along First Avenue, initially to protect the trees, but also to provide irrigation water. We installed vertical pipes that doubled as tree guards and a detention water system. A perforated section of pipe in the soil slowly irrigated the young trees. Objects such as crutches and bed frames, both from the abandoned single resident occupant hotels, served as a cost-effective, ad hoc solution, and illustrated a neighborhood in transition. The bed frames protecting the trees lasted a number of years until the thin metal head and foot frames rusted or were damaged while protecting the trees from automobiles. The bed frames were later transformed from relics into artifacts. We made a mold of the bed frames and cast them in iron. They are installed at locations where the transition continues.

COMPOSTING COMMODE

In 1978, a *Composting Commode* was installed on First Avenue in response to continued indiscriminant street level defecation and as a counterpart to a regional expansion of unsustainable flush technology. The commode sat over future tree pits and when full would be moved up the street to start anew. It had been our experience when planting trees that most of the soil was comprised of hard pan clay. Use of the commode

Bed Frame Tree Guard protecting an elm tree

enhanced the soil. The commode was designed as a stoop toilet with an aeration system for decomposing. There was an interior railing to assist patrons and a twenty-foot solar draw ventilation pipe, which was notched at the top to function as an adjustable wind pipe organ.

Obtaining a street use permit would have been a protracted affair, so in the spirit of a "temporary prototype" the commode was camouflaged within a shell of an off-the-shelf portable self-contained chemical toilet to avoid unnecessary attention by the authorities. The theory was that portable chemical toilets were part of the urban visual landscape, but a composting toilet that looked like an outhouse would be a red flag. Patrons, primarily the homeless, had no problem accepting the facility during its short existence at two locations.

Detail of dogwood planting after *Composting Commode* is moved

The authorities eventually discovered the ruse of the Composting Commode and requested its removal. We agreed to work together to address the issues this intervention dramatized, the basic human need for decent public facilities. The commode found a new home at a community garden adjacent to an alternative pubic school. The attention attracted the university architecture department to conduct a weeklong workshop in downtown Seattle to address the issues this project raised.

THE BELLTOWN PAN

Around the early 1980s, the Belltown Café at 2309 First Avenue became the social hearth for the community. The proprietors often did exchanges of food for art and one trade was for the concept and fabrication of the Belltown Pan. The pan was designed as a large cooking pan in the shape of a bell and sized to fit in a commercial oven. The pan was made from sheet copper, riveted together and tinned on the inside. Most of the year it hung from a bracket outside the café and functioned as a sign. On Groundhog Day, the pan was taken down, cleaned, and a large assortment of roots such as rutabaga, parsnips, beets, carrots, onions, potatoes, and garlic were prepared and baked.

Details of Belltown
pan and root pie

The connection to the root-consuming groundhog was a metaphor signaling the end of the winter when the roots in the root cellar were running out and we were anticipating the coming of spring. A piece of the pie sold for 99 cents and the event grew as an informal celebration over the few years of the pan's use. The café closed later in the 1980s and the building was torn down for new construction. There is a restaurant occupying the location and preparations are being made to return the pan to the facade and the yearly celebration to the community.

WATER TABLE/WATER GLASS

Some new construction along First Avenue has extended the episodic experience to include common areas and plazas. One such project was the *Water Table/ Water Glass*. This project redirected the roof watershed down to the publicly accessible plaza and into two sculptures. One element is a large drinking glass with a straw connected to the downspout. The other plaza element is a water table with an adjoining roof watershed. A downspout is connected to a table through the fourth leg. The ten-story head

top: View of the
public plaza with
Water Table / Water Glass

bottom: *Water Table*
expressing the rainfall
head of water

of water is expressed up through the pierced text "water." The word "table" is sandblasted and has an ephemeral quality that changes when the black granite table surface is wet or dry. Rainwater from both sculptures supplies a landscape and then charges a cistern below before recirculation. This wetlands planting project will require an engaged residential community to eventually succeed.

GROWING VINE STREET

We began the Growing Vine Street Project by defining the word "green" in relation to environmental sustainability rather than to traditional landscaping. This part of the city was "plumbed" to dispose of rain from roofs and hard surfaces through an antiquated combined sanitary and storm system. We proposed to redirect this urban watershed and keep it at the surface as an asset rather than a liability flushed out of sight. We have put the city on notice that we see gray water and brown water as the next opportunity.

The design team developed a working logic that equated the street to a crack. We needed to build a structural armature based on street infrastructure, site conditions, ownership, easements, as well as community and business needs. Rather than fighting the infrastructure, we let it reveal itself by working with the existing conditions and taking the path of least resistance. It was a pragmatic approach given the limited funding. Our design mitigated and nurtured the streetscape with the urban watershed through an interconnected system of green roofs, cisterns, detention planters, and street watercourses we called runnels, which are intended as an extension of the urban crack. The watershed journey is episodic and transparent as it makes its way down the eight sloping blocks of Vine Street towards Puget Sound. This project requires the patience of seven generations. We provided a start that will hopefully instill a desire to integrate similar systems in future development.

Maintaining community engagement during protracted consensus, permitting, and implementation processes is important. Private and public-sector processes are often too lengthy for the collective memory of a community. One approach to keeping the community engaged is to borrow lessons from First Avenue—the temporary prototype and other spontaneous interventions. The *Skyway Seed Bank* was one such project.

SKYWAY SEEDBANK

For over 50 years, a water tower platform, resting on the roof of the abandoned Skyway Luggage factory at Elliot Avenue and Vine Street, had nurtured a unique landscape of volunteer grasses and mosses in less than five inches of self-generated soil. We recognized that this repository could provide a seed stock for future neighborhood green roofs. This landscape was a survivor specific to the ecosystem of this particular urban environment. Segments of this seed bank were transplanted into recycled suitcases, referencing the Skyway Luggage Building that hosted the seed bank

above: *Skyway Seedbank* on the roof of the Skyway Luggage building

right: *Portable Landscapes* at the Henry Art Gallery, 2000

on its factory roof. The suitcases were also a symbol of a neighborhood in demographic transition. The suitcase planters were fixed to pallets to make them portable. These were placed along the eight blocks of Vine Street where they waited to be adopted by the community. The suitcases suggested displacement and hope as they lay themselves open exposing their contents to the whims of community and government.

In an attempt to soften the impact of suitcases with the Seed Bank of volunteer "ugly weeds" and their intended use as a seed

dispersal system for future green roofs, the lower tier of the two-tier pallet of suitcases were planted with petunias and pansies and a covering of beauty bark, to exemplify the suburban coding for beauty. The planters were on the street for two years with the hope that residents would begin to adopt them. These suitcase planter locations were recipients of various levels of community engagement. One member of the business community, who failed to grasp the concept, forced the city to require a street use permit, causing their removal. Temporary prototypes should not require street use permits. I complied with the removal of all but one. Out of sight of this individual's scrutiny, re-germination awaits another day.

Barrel planters on Alaskan Way at Vine Street

At about the same time, two installations consisting of 55-gallon steel barrels strapped to fabricated steel pallets and galvanize-dipped as a single unit were sited and planted along the freight train tracks at the foot of Vine Street. The barrels referenced the warehouse activity of what was once a working waterfront adjacent to a salmon cannery on Vine Street. A community member has adopted one set. The other has become a recipient of vagabond plantings, perhaps seeds borne from the passing freight cars. Unlike the suitcase planters, the barrels on skids were out of the way and less interventionist in appearance, thus more acceptable. There was one complaint to the Port Authority of "illegal dumping" by someone who assumed the installation was an indiscriminant dumping of old barrels, perhaps full of toxins.

BECKONING CISTERN AND CISTERN STEPS

Interventions and temporary prototypes provide a visible and engaging presence for ideas. This helps keep the community engaged for a time when collective consensus is needed to support more ambitious projects. Collaborations with the city and the private development sector require a consistent and dedicated group of community advocates. Two recent projects along Vine Street exemplify this dedication of time, patience, and collaborative spirit, and reinforce the Growing Vine Street mission of roof watershed diversion to a cistern and landscape. One, *Beckoning Cistern*, has been completed. Construction began on the other, *Cistern Steps*, in the summer of 2004. This process has taken over four years because of the city's hesitation in approving innovation. These two projects relied heavily on private developers with courage and belief in the principles of Growing Vine Street. It is imperative that future private development along Vine Street follows the example set particularly at 81 Vine Street.

Beckoning Cistern at 81 Vine Street demystifies the journey of water in an urban watershed as rainwater travels from roof to bow truss downspouts to eighty-foot-long detention planters and finally, to two more downspouts. One downspout supports a series of vertical landscape detention planter devices and the other downspout offers rainwater to the Beckoning Cistern. The

top: *Beckoning Cistern*

bottom: Lower pools of *Beckoning Cistern*

cistern is a large 10 foot by 6 foot diameter tank, as if a sleeve, with a hand and extended index finger reaching out to the down spout. It mimics the gesture of the painting in the Sistine Chapel of Adam and God with their fingers about to touch. In this case, God is the downspout implying Mother Nature as the alternate deity. The tank water overflow pours out the tip of the thumb and into a set of planters where a variety of native wetland plantings have established themselves. The tank water is available for additional watering as determined by the residence. In the next block down the hill, Cistern Steps is to receive additional waters from an adjacent condominium roof and direct it into a series of stepped wetland planters, rather than send the water into the sewer. The Cistern Steps is located adjacent to the Belltown P-Patch and is considered an extension of it. One more block and the water reaches Puget Sound.

The challenge is to bring in natural systems by retrofitting the city. The diverse talents and inventive approaches individuals bring to the collaboration benefit the entire community. The goal is to build a social network to realize the full potential of Vine Street.

Buster would like to thank the following people for their work and support on the First Avenue Streetscape Project: Denny Regrade Community Council; The initial design team—Jack Mackie, Joan Paulson, Deborah Reinheart, Paul Reinheart, and Ann Hershey; Department of Neihborhoods; Seattle Engineering; Marvin Black and Shane DeWald, City Arborist; Walter White, Belltown Pan coppersmith; Barbara Goldstein, Seattle Arts Commission 1978–2004; and many more over the years. www.bustersimpson.net

Making Their Own Plans

CITY REPAIR

RESOURCE CENTER

PARK FICTION

CAN MASDEU

EDITORS
Brett Bloom
Ava Bromberg

WHITEWALLS EDITOR
Anthony Elms

DESIGN
Department of Graphic Sciences

Belltown Paradise/Making Their Own Plans (ISBN 0-945323-05-0) was compiled by
Brett Bloom and Ava Bromberg who work together as In the Field.
www.inthefield.info

Published by WhiteWalls, Inc., a not-for-profit corporation,
P.O. Box 8204, Chicago, Illinois 60680

Funding for the production and publication of this book comes from
The City of Seattle's Office of Art and Cultural Affairs
and Seattle City Light % for Art Funds.

Contributions and gifts to WhiteWalls, Inc., are tax-deductible to the extent allowed by law.
This publication is supported in part by grants from the Illinois Arts Council,
a state agency; by a CityArts grant from the City of Chicago Department
of Cultural Affairs; and by our friends and subscribers. WhiteWalls, Inc., is a member
of the Illinois Arts Alliance and the National Association of Artists Organizations.

IMAGES ON COVER
top: Fireworks at Can Masdeu
bottom: Sunnyside Piazza, City Repair

Table of Contents

Introduction

It is not easy to reconfigure an undemocratic, polluted, gentrifying city into a more just and livable place. It takes considerable effort to recognize the immensity of the problems, no less see clearly where the work begins. Cities around the world increasingly lack decent affordable housing, public spaces not controlled by private interests, and cultural spaces free from corporate influence. Replacing bureaucracy and top-down urban planning with inclusive neighborhood-led design is imperative. This cannot be entrusted to architects and planning professionals trained in various economies of space.

Projects that change the urban landscape without deferring to precedent or city mandates were the inspiration for this book. The work presented here is by no means exhaustive, yet there is much to learn from these groups and organizations. They are immersed in struggles to creatively reshape their neighborhoods and cities. We asked them to write about their experiences. The contributors are City Repair, Portland; The Resource Center, Chicago; Park Fiction, Hamburg; Can Masdeu, Barcelona. Each offers distinct strategies for self-organizing and creatively impacting a neighborhood. Their initiatives teach us about the cities and cultures they are from while offering ways to overcome seemingly insurmountable bureaucracy and social stagnation. Each deals with the city in a different way. They all use creativity, compassion, and action to realize different realities and challenge the status quo. This is necessary if we are to create more open and participatory societies for future generations to further transform.

Beyond the limited scope of trickle-down urban planning and its pseudo-participatory processes are living neighborhoods where democracy thrives and people have a say in how their environment is shaped. We cannot trust experts to design cities for us. We can learn a lot about how cities work from the people who live in and use them, but it is all too rare that inhabitants are asked how they would like their cities to be. The contributors to this book do not wait to be asked to act on their desires. They organize themselves, and implement the changes they want to see.

far left:
City Repair's
Share-It Square

···

In the summer of 2003, we met with Mark Lakeman, part of Portland-based City Repair. He eloquently explained a major component of the group's activities: getting people to "unplug from the grid." Anyone familiar with the terminology used by advocates of "green" technology, such as making houses out of natural materials or using solar energy, knows this as a cliché that means taking oneself out of the loop of un-renewable, wasteful building and energy consumption. This is not, however, how Lakeman was using the phrase. He was talking about a much older grid, the Roman Empire's system for mapping out entire nations, articulating a massive political and social structure from the ultimate position of power and detachment. This same approach was used by early planners in the United States to map out vast tracts of land that would not be populated for decades, if not centuries. This centralized and reductive system, Lakeman explained, still pre-determines the way neighborhoods in the U.S. look and feel, and the kinds of community spaces they have, and do not have, before anyone actually moves in.

Such a restrictive design is maintained for easy governance and control. Inherited structures like this are not only obsolete they are socially corrosive. Yet, when we collectively assert our desire to build a park or tend a garden, when we work with others to make something larger than personal economic interests or private property, we challenge such unimaginative and oppressive structures. We create new social configurations and local places tuned to our needs. We show what human beings are capable of when we work together. Building community in any landscape is difficult; divergent visions, disagreements, and other pressures can greatly interfere with collective efforts, but working through them can be a source of democratic strength.

Our meeting with Mark Lakeman was at Sunnyside Piazza, one of City Repair's most developed neighborhood sites that has transformed an intersection of two streets into a public square. It is no longer a place just for cars; it has become too visually disorienting to drive through quickly. Everything has been brought

back to relate to the human body, its speed, and sense of time. This was immediately tangible. It is difficult to convey this experience to anyone who has not visited this particular place. We felt so comfortable in this intersection that we lay down in the middle of the giant painted sunflower that filled it. We felt safe to soak up the sun's rays and enjoy what has to be one of the most incredible experiences of public space we have ever had.

We had similarly intense, yet vastly different, experiences with the work of the other contributors to this book. It is extremely important to see their work together, and share it widely. We would like to thank them all for their ideas, actions, and generosity.

—Brett Bloom and Ava Bromberg

The City Repair Project

BY STUART COWAN, MARK LAKEMAN, JENNY LEIS,
DANIEL LERCH AND JAN C. SEMENZA

The City Repair Project is a non-profit organization based in Portland, Oregon, born out of a grassroots initiative that legally converted a street intersection into a neighborhood public square. We involve hundreds of volunteers and activists working on public gatherings and events to make our communities better places to live. City Repair's work is inspired by the idea that localization—of culture, economy, decision-making—is a necessary foundation for a more community-oriented and ecologically sustainable society.

The volunteer executive staff shares responsibilities in a non-hierarchical and consensus decision-making model. City Repair is an excellent example of a chaordic ("chaotically ordered") organization. A chaordic organization serves to enable the periphery—where people are deeply engaged with hands-on community actions—by providing resources and delegating decision-making. Chaordic processes prevent the accumulation of power and resources in any one part of the organization while maintaining a remarkable level of coherence and creativity. City Repair is a living organism, which in turn reminds the city that it is a confederation of villages, and awakens each village to its role as a living system embedded in broader ecosystems.

OUR MISSION: The City Repair Project is an organized group action that educates and inspires communities and individuals to creatively transform the places where they live. We facilitate artistic and ecologically-oriented placemaking through projects that honor the interconnection of human communities and the natural world.

PLACEMAKING

City Repair's work is based on the idea of "Placemaking," which is the creation of a place whose structure and use is determined by the people who inhabit that place. Great urban places serve many functions and are continuously adapted to the local culture and environment. As the process of developing a community place proceeds, people develop deeper relationships with each other and their surroundings, literally creating a common

far left top: Community celebration at Share-It Square

far left bottom: Sellwood Moonday T-Hows

ground that empowers people to transcend differences, creatively address civic affairs, and continue building upon their shared public places.

CITY REPAIR PROJECTS:

Sellwood Moonday T-Hows (1996): A semi-permanent gathering environment modeled after ancestral European and indigenous meeting houses. A successful adaptation of function that provided the local community impetus to establish a permanent public gathering place.

T-Horse Mobile Neighborhood Public Square (1996 to present): A mobile teahouse and public gathering place that travels to different Portland neighborhoods providing a comfortable, creative atmosphere where people can meet their neighbors and form community bonds.

T-Horse Mobile
Public Square

Intersection Repair (1996 to present): A community-driven transformation of street intersections into neighborhood public squares. As of January 2004, six Intersection Repair projects are in existence and dozens of new projects are underway nationwide.

Hands Around Portland (1997-2000): A city-scale human circle of approximately 7,000 people, this project is a gesture of hope, community, and human interconnectedness.

Portland Public Place Master Plan (2000): A five-year plan to help Portland's 96 neighborhoods each create at least one public square.

Earth Day Celebration of Localization (2000 to present): This annual festival of all things local highlights the resources of our interconnected human communities and our environments, and the sheer beauty of public gathering.

Community Visioning (2001 to present): Workshops that assist residents, businesses, and visitors of an inner-city commercial street (SE Division), a neighborhood (Sunnyside), and a coastal Oregon town (Bay City) to envision sustainable placemaking opportunities.

Village Building Convergence (2002 to present): An annual ten-day event that reclaims urban spaces and transforms them into community places. Daytime hands-on workshops and evening events teach, inspire, and bring together thousands of people in local communities.

PLACEMAKING IN OUR NEIGHBORHOODS: INTERSECTION REPAIR

In Portland, as with cities across the nation, many neighborhood streets are desolate and anonymous, torn apart by speeding traffic. There is little to inspire conversation, creativity, democracy, community gatherings, reflections of local culture, a sense of safety, or even local economic vitality. Intersection Repair reclaims the crossing of pathways—the historical place of gathering—and turns it back to the community. Intersection Repair projects are guided by the direct participation and leadership of a neighborhood to determine a shared vision for a neighborhood gathering place, create the designs and functions, collect the materials needed, and then build, manage, and celebrate each other and the neighborhood.

> Public places, plazas, lively streets, friendly exchange between passers-by, shared sense of ownership, food, kids, laughter, music, art, culture—where have our "village hearts" gone?

CONTEXT OF INTERSECTION REPAIR

Town commons have traditionally been the geographical glue that binds a community together. In 1785, the Continental Congress passed the National Land Ordinance, which estab-

lished a continental grid plan over all lands west of the Ohio River and practically guaranteed that public squares would be absent from new American cities. Much of the source and nature of our social isolation and urban tragedies result from this; we have few commons to facilitate collective understanding, vision, or responsibility.

Public gathering places are essential components for building vibrant neighborhood communities. Without these places, where does the daily practice of community happen? Often, throughout the nation, it simply does not. Intersection Repair is a process for reclaiming our identity as neighbors and returning public squares—the heart of community—to our neighborhoods, one by one.

HOW IT WORKS

Intersection Repair projects happen with support and facilitation assistance from City Repair. The initial neighborhood "sparks" reach out to their neighbors and invite everyone to learn more about the possibilities of building a neighborhood center. The initial steps are critical and should include: hosting social gatherings, encouraging conversation in a general way about the neighborhood, and simply spending time in public places. These are the moments when individuals feel personally welcomed and engaged to share their talents and opinions in this neighborhood effort. "Social capital" is built, and the neighborhood as a whole takes ownership of the concept of re-building shared public places.

The designs for the public square are created by the neighborhood through a series of

INTERSECTION REPAIR provides a way for citizens to reclaim the identities of our communities and return public squares to our neighborhoods.

THE PROJECTS:

• Increase communication and interaction between neighbors

• Reinterpret existing public spaces and adapt them to establish a site and a framework for cooperation and local participation in community affairs

• Provide a focus for neighborhood identity and culture, providing a place for activities such as news sharing, tool lending, celebrations, and spontaneous conversation.

• Beautify the public environment, can lower crime rates and reduce traffic speed.

community workshops. The process usually begins with an assessment of the current neighborhood needs and assets, culture and history, common interests, local climate, ecology, and topography. The neighborhood then formulates a vision and a set of strategies to meet their goals. With scores of people involved in the decision-making, it usually requires compromise and creative solutions to find a suitable design. The strongest and most interesting concepts result from the process of addressing each person's concerns, opinions, and ideas.

While the projects are physical, the essence of an Intersection Repair is unseen to the eye. Behind the community kiosks, benches, and street murals lies an awakened neighborhood that has come together and created conversations. This placemaking is as much about psychological ownership and reclamation of relationships as it is about a place. Placemaking reminds us that we still share common interests and the power to manifest them.

The projects evolve in phases, naturally unfolding from time people spend together in their own neighborhood. Many groups start with something small and do-able so that the community can accomplish it together and engender a common basis for potential next steps. Each phase of the project is punctuated by moments of celebration and reflection.

The City of Portland allows street painting and construction in the right of way, according to City Ordinance #175937 (September 19, 2001). The Portland Department of Transportation (PDOT) has established a precedent for these projects by granting revocable permits for ongoing intersection modifications. A petition of support is required by the city; the petition has signatures from each of the adjacent residents and at least 80% of the residents on the project street frontage(s) within two standard city blocks of the proposed project. The residents have to provide a written description of the proposed changes, including drawings depicting how the intersection will look when completed. With support from PDOT, the residents demonstrate how the project will improve, or at least maintain, traffic safety and the safety of individuals at or in the vicinity of the intersection.

Each neighbor is encouraged to contribute their ideas, desires and resources and cultivate their own interests in this participatory process. People also develop partnerships with

neighborhood associations, government agencies, local businesses, schools, and organizations that are all working toward similar goals of healthy, livable communities. Intersection Repair simply becomes a mechanism for working together.

Funding for these projects comes from a variety of sources. Once people feel that they are part of an exciting neighborhood process, their spirit of resourcefulness and generosity is engaged. Many neighborhoods find ample materials in their backyards or garages, and local businesses are often pleased to donate materials, food, or funds. Neighborhood groups also write grants, host creative fundraising events, and seek resourceful partnerships. Overall, the projects cost a fraction of the value they generate.

The Portland City Council and Department of Transportation support Intersection Repair because it improves neighborhood livability and engages citizens in participatory democracy without spending a single tax dollar. Projects are permitted in communities who prove widespread support for the designs. Therefore, the community has decision-making power over what they want in their neighborhood as long as they work together. The process is continuously evolving as neighborhoods generate new ideas for their public places.

Intersection Repairs touch upon issues that transcend political, cultural, and economic lines. These foundations allow us to determine our own destiny together as a community. Many people find personal meaning in these projects as they are deeply transformational and a lot of fun! Each project plants invaluable seeds for the future.

HISTORY OF INTERSECTION REPAIR: THE SHARE-IT SQUARE

The Intersection Repair concept first developed out of a creative, insurrectionary action by a single neighborhood to reclaim public space at their most local street intersection. Since the initial prototype, "Intersection Repair" has become a household term in Portland, referring to the restoration process of re-engaging people at nodes where historically people's lives would have intersected.

In the spring of 1996, people in Portland's Sellwood neighborhood began holding tea parties in a beautiful, temporary gathering place built by a neighbor in a garden of fruit trees and flowers. This special place, known as the "T-Hows," was based upon a simple idea: given the opportunity to share time and drink with each other in a comfortable, free place, people will come together and start to build relationships, as their ancestors used to in their own meeting places.

Labyrinth Piazza

It worked. Soon, hundreds of neighbors were coming to the gatherings. Music, dancing, poetry readings and, of course, tea, flowed freely as friendships formed. Neighbors who had lived near each other for years but never met came to know and care about each other.

Because the T-Hows was built without asking permission, the local Bureau of Buildings issued a directive to remove it. However, hundreds of neighbors, architecture and engineering firms across the city, and even the media objected! Momentum began to shift and people found the courage to create an even bolder concept for community self-development. This time it was in the nearby street intersection.

continued on page 18

CASE STUDY: The Sunnyside Piazza

When I moved into the Sunnyside neighborhood in Portland, OR in 1999, I was stunned by the magnitude of urban problems including heroin, crack, and alcohol abuse literally in my backyard. The neighborhood was plagued by social disorder, crime, and vandalism. I soon realized that it was particularly excessive on Wednesdays and Fridays when a local soup kitchen served the homeless a warm meal. The soup kitchen had fallen down on its responsibility to monitor crime and substance abuse at its events. Yet, how could anyone argue against a soup kitchen? We decided to tackle these issues by using the same community organizing tool: food. We started having regular brunch meetings with all the neighbors to discuss creative approaches to neighborhood stewardship.

During nine months of meetings, discussions, workshops, design plans, outreach and block parties the community conceived of a plan to paint an intersection. While the benefits to the community of painting the streets seemed obvious to me, others pointed out that the streets exist to be driven on. With a considerable amount of outreach and mediation we were able to appease the concerns of the skeptics. The community painted a large sunflower in the middle of the intersection and we arguably created the most beautiful intersection in town. The pattern resembles two spirals, mirror images of each other, and mathematically represents a Fibonacci series, a pattern found in many natural phenomena, including sunflowers. We inaugurated the Sunnyside Piazza on September 22, 2001, with a big party including residents and homeless alike.

After another nine months of preparations a second phase of community art was realized. A cob art-wall was built with colorful mosaics, shapes, and niches. A cob information kiosk was installed for exchanging messages and notices intended to facilitate social interactions. A solar-powered fountain tiled with

glass mosaics was constructed to invite passersby to pause to the sound of running water and to interact with each other. More structures were soon to follow with large trellises on all corners for hanging gardens.

The Sunnyside Piazza has become a destination for pedestrians and a place for people to meet. We have evidence that this successful example of community organizing has had a beneficial impact on social networks and well-being. Crime data suggest that there has been a significant decrease in reported offenses. These data vindicate the merits of public participation in urban design with cost-effective benefits to the community.

—Jan C. Semenza

continued from page 15

First, a group of neighbors created a plan to claim the street intersection as shared place by painting the asphalt, and approached the Portland Office of Transportation (PDOT) about the project. PDOT refused the idea, some of the neighbors even being told, "That's public space—so no one can use it!"

At the same time, other individuals within PDOT advised the neighbors that the only way to get the city to even consider such an untried idea was to just initiate it without permission. The neighbors refined the design and decided to practice civil disobedience installing the "Intersection Repair" without city

Memorial to a cyclist killed in a traffic accident

approval. In September 1996, they arranged for a legal block party street closure on all four streets converging at SE 9th and Sherrett. During the community event they installed the first phase of "Share-it Square."

Share-it Square began as a series of colorful painted concentric circles graphically connecting the four corners of the intersection. It also included permanent structures on each corner representing the kinds of functions that are found in public squares, such as a bulletin board and information kiosk, a 24-hour tea-serving station (the community "watering hole"), and a playhouse. The intention was to mark the intersection as a shared place for the development of neighborhood culture and creative engagement where vehicles and pedestrians would be able to safely share space.

Immediately, PDOT sent notification to remove the installation and threatened to fine the neighbors involved. The

neighborhood group then engaged PDOT and city council members in dialogue about the project, and set out to prove its value by surveying the neighborhood and observing behavior at the intersection. The resulting survey showed that the vast majority of respondents perceived increases in neighborhood communication and safety, decreases in crime activity and in traffic speed.

The project quickly won city support when officials realized that the project was meeting a host of city livability goals without costing tax dollars. The city council began a series of ordinances that granted permits to the project, and set out guidelines for similar projects to be installed throughout Portland.

Over the next few years, the neighbors refined and added elements to their Intersection Repair: the 24-hour tea station was rebuilt with steel, wood, concrete, and mosaic; the bulletin board was expanded with a plexiglas roof and chalk boards; a produce-sharing station and a sidewalk chalk dispenser appeared. Many more amenities such as benches made from cob (an adobe-like natural building material made of clay, straw, sand, and water), communication stations, and other structures have emerged. The intersection mural has been redesigned and repainted multiple times.

The impact on the neighborhood as a whole has been profound. The concentration of families with children and others with a pronounced community orientation wanting to live together near Share-It Square is evidence of the impact. Social capacity has increased, inspiring many side projects and relationships. Personal benefits include expanded social networks, a stronger sense of local identity, less neighborhood conflict, and innumerable opportunities for creative engagement.

SYNCHRONICITY:
THE VILLAGE BUILDING CONVERGENCE

Intersection Repair projects on their own are momentous events, but when a dozen projects are synchronized, the whole city feels the impact. The Village Building Convergence (VBC) is an annual ten-day period of action, education, and celebration grounded by building dozens of new community gathering

places. The combined power of simultaneously transforming spaces into places in neighborhood nodes across the city creates a sense of reclaiming our city as a collection of coordinated village centers.

Because the VBC is a synchronization of multiple projects, the impact is greater than any individual undertaking. The project not only utilizes resources and ideas more efficiently, it also makes a profound statement of the community's collective visions. Thousands of people participate in the ten-day work party. Evening events with visionary innovators and leaders spark dialogue about creating sustainable urban villages within the modern city. Daytime workshops and shared meals become times for conversation and connection.

The overall event trains developing leaders and builds capacity for individuals and communities, while offering us an experience of actually living in an urban village. The VBC becomes ten days of inhabiting a timely vision: working as a community to better ourselves, learn from each other, laugh, reflect, and dance. There is an infectious air of possibility during those ten days.

Village Building Convergence Internal Structure

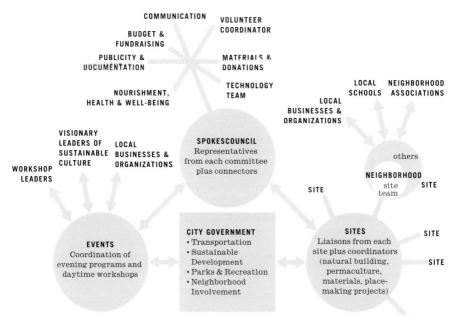

LIVING FRACTALS:
COMMUNICATION AND COORDINATION

Beyond any built projects resulting from the Village Building Convergence, an equally historic and innovative organizational structure is created. The VBC can be described as a scaled series of fractals: a repeating form of localized empowerment that is coordinated to take action at many levels. The efficiency of the model is based on consciously negotiating between the community vision and each person or group's interest. People are therefore able to feel in control of their work, have ample resources and support, and contribute to a meaningful combined accomplishment. The VBC is coordinated by hundreds of volunteers: neighbors, activists, professionals, students, and other community organizers, as well as its sponsors: The City Repair Project, Southeast Uplift Neighborhood Coalition, and KBOO Community Radio.

A "spokescouncil" comprised of representatives of each committee guides the overall project and serves as the hub coordinating body. Each committee is empowered to make the majority of their own decisions, but brings significant matters to the spokescouncil.

This structure allows many people to be the decision-makers, dispersing the power and responsibilities among the community. This model also teaches people how to communicate effectively within a complex organism and truly work as a team. With an understanding that everybody has different working styles and interests, people synchronize efforts in order to accomplish great feats beyond individual capability.

VBC PROCESS FOR COMPLETING
SIMULTANEOUS PROJECTS

The fractal model of organization can extend beyond the internal structure of the VBC. It allows for multiple partnerships citywide by identifying specific links among many layers of the organization. For example, the VBC 2003 partnered with five city bureaus, dozens of local businesses and organizations, schools, neighborhood associations, and hundreds of volunteers.

City Repair has developed a step-by-step process in order to simultaneously implement several neighborhood en-

hancement projects throughout the city. The neighborhoods are the focus of the process, and the VBC provides coordination, facilitation, process, and technical support. The process begins with VBC organizers announcing via local media the opportunity to support new neighborhood enhancement projects. Interested community members then reach out to their neighborhoods to gauge the potential. If interested, the neighborhood groups follow the Intersection Repair model of community involvement and design. To gain support as a project of the VBC, the neighborhood answers a survey about their motivation, level of neighborhood participation, and vision. The VBC identifies projects to support based on available resources to meet each neighborhood's projected needs.

The VBC organizers assist each neighborhood by working with their neighbors to develop their designs, acquire materials for the projects, and complete the city permitting process. Throughout the process, neighborhood identity and ownership of the projects supersedes that of City Repair and the VBC; City

Flow-diagram of Community Empowerment through Urban Form by the City Repair Project

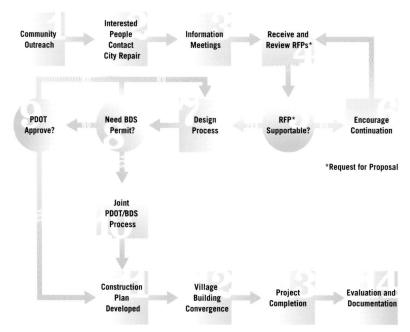

Community Outreach → Interested People Contact City Repair → Information Meetings → Receive and Review RFPs*

PDOT Approve? ← Need BDS Permit? ← Design Process ← RFP* Supportable? → Encourage Continuation

*Request for Proposal

Joint PDOT/BDS Process

Construction Plan Developed → Village Building Convergence → Project Completion → Evaluation and Documentation

Repair organizers serve as facilitators and project support only when requested.

During the Village Building Convergence each May, the neighborhoods and VBC participants showcase this model of neighborhood improvement by working together, celebrating and building new places in their streets.

ACTING LOCALLY AND GLOBALLY: COOPERATION

With the VBC and our neighborhood associations, Portland, Oregon, is leading the nation in re-envisioning civic infrastructure. We are learning in Portland that localization of culture, economy, and decision-making is the foundation for a sustainable future. The Village Building Convergence is about actively building community capacity, and realizing the strength and beauty of our power. The VBC is a statement of our collective dedication to create a world of cooperation.

The City Repair Project promotes events and activities that inspire people to take active, direct roles in re-creating their neighborhoods and cities. This model of community involvement in urban design has tangible benefits to both residents and non-residents, and has sparked projects city and nationwide. These projects of localization dynamically connect individuals to plan and implement creative and attractive urban places that enrich their quality of life.

How to Make a City Farm

AS TOLD BY KEN DUNN TO SALEM COLLO-JULIN

Empty parcels of city land should be cleared, cultivated, and turned into economically and socially productive urban farms. I think if an investment were made into urban agriculture, full employment would enter communities where there is little, nutrition would be improved for everyone, and a mission would emerge—neighbors would contribute to the health and wealth of the city.

The Resource Center, our Chicago-based group that runs City Farm, started 30 years ago. We saw resources being wasted. We thought that these resources, if captured and used creatively, could be an element of building a higher quality of life.

Since then, we have become convinced that the entire dominant economy and culture is our enemy. We have to invent an alternative sustaining economy. When inventing this new economy, we try to refrain from participating in the other economy as much as possible, by moving toward producing our own "whatever." This includes producing our own food.

Growing food means growing yourself—it is all part of a sustainable system. The dominant food system is quite unsustainable right now. Its production methods harm the environment consuming hydrocarbons and chemicals. The planet suffers, the farm workers that must use this machinery suffer, and residents at the dinner table end up harming themselves. This is why we feel that new food systems need to be developed.

I think that it is not obvious to everybody that our economy and political system is broken. However, more people are becoming aware that our food system is broken. Chemical agriculture is not good for the planet, the farm workers, or us.

So we sought an alternative, instead of trying to reform a broken system. It is a revolution of orienting people properly to the things they consume—introducing them to their own food system. The ideal is that people grow their own food. If they cannot do it themselves, they should at least know who did, and keep everything as local as possible. That is the context in which we view urban agriculture.

far left: Ken Dunn at the City Farm
Photo, Rorke Johnson

City Farm is one of the Resource Center's sustainable organic farms. It is in between Cabrini Green and the Gold Coast, the former, a place with many vacant lots and the latter, a place with resources to spare. We grow thirty varieties of tomatoes, beets, carrots, potatoes, lettuces, herbs, and melons. We sell the food from City Farm to the public, but our primary sales are to local chefs. Places like the restaurant at the Ritz-Carlton and the Frontera Grill like our tomatoes. So do we. The compost we use comes from restaurants we sell to, thus completing the cycle.

When I first came to Chicago, I was a graduate student, but very much aware that the university was not a place where one could find all the solutions. It seemed so strange that the city was so full of things that needed to be done and so full of people that needed something to do. Nobody was making the connection between them.

I was a graduate student in philosophy and I gave myself a test problem. If you are any good at philosophy, you can figure out what to do about this. I focused on the most external problem—people needing something to do, and things needing to be done.

This was thirty years ago. The first project that occurred to me: cans and bottles that were being thrown out by everybody on vacant lots and streets could in fact be income for individuals if we established a location that would buy from them. This buyback was my first project.

On most corners, there were guys drinking and throwing their empty bottles into vacant lots. So one weekend, I borrowed a Volkswagen from a friend and got some garbage cans and told these guys, "I have an idea. Work with me. Let us pick up all these bottles here and put them in these garbage cans. I will go sell them to the glass plant, and then I will come back in a couple of hours and we will split up the cash." And so they did it. I came back and paid them something like $2.90 each—it was not much.

I was just pleased, as an academic, that I had devised a successful project. And as I was walking away, one of them said, "Uh, where do we work on Monday?" I spun around, and thought a very academic reply, "No, you do not understand. I am just providing ideas, not solutions." But I could not say that. So I just sort

of stood blankly for a few seconds, and then I said, "I will get back to you."

So I went back. I did not want to go out with a van and do this thing all the time. I wanted something that was commensurate with the problem—that was more than just me. I put together a schedule of times and locations and distributed copies to the guys. At 9:00 on Saturday morning, I would be at this corner, and at 9:30, I would be four blocks away. I established a route around the community that they would all know, and they could pass out the schedules to all of their friends.

I went out and bought a larger truck and a scale, and I ended up bringing $200 worth of bottles to the plant on the first day. It was a success. There really was a willing group of collectors. There were plenty of bottles. And that was the first embodiment of the Resource Center. This program continues under contract with the City of Chicago and the Chicago Housing Authority.

While I was still a student, I spent my Saturdays running this route, until I realized that running the route could be a regular job. So I hired one of the guys that had been very responsible. And he was the

first employee of the Resource Center. You see, that is the basic concept. Is there a human resource that is overlooked or wasted? Is there a material resource that is overlooked or wasted? And can there be a connection between the two?

The City Farm with Cabrini Green in the background
Photo, Rorke Johnson

Pleased with having devised this, I started to think, okay, now what do we have? A clean, vacant lot. And that is a material resource. Is there a population appropriate to that? There

were a lot of retired or unemployed people in the communities that hosted these vacant lots. I tried to think of ways of bringing them together.

The first thing that occurred to me would be to farm these lots. We could not just throw plants in the earth, though. You want to enrich the soil first, but how do you do it? We did not want to go to Monsanto or other chemical companies for chemical fertilizers. We wanted to think organic. We started collecting weeds and grass and other organic materials and started a compost site.

It is true that doing compost instead of buying chemicals was an outgrowth of having no budget. However, in my child-

Tomatoes, fresh from the City Farm
Photo, Rorke Johnson

hood, our family had farms. I am a native to Kansas. I ran the family farm for a few years, before I decided that mechanized agriculture, with chemicals, was just wrong. At the time I did not yet know what was right.

I began helping on the family farm in 1948. Things were natural and organic then. Then the forces of more mechanization and more payments to the bank appeared. We had to buy chemical fertilizers and then we had to spray to protect our investment. I started before commercial agriculture, or corporate agriculture, tried to take over. While working on the farm, I

introduced mechanization and chemicals to keep the farm viable in our dominant economy. And then I realized we have gotten away from responsible use of the soil.

My dad got our farm soon after he left high school from the bank for almost nothing because it had really been destroyed and nobody could farm it. Rows of trees 30 feet tall were in a dune. My first years of farming were spent bringing health back to the farm. We did it by getting stands of alfalfa and clover established.

I came to questioning chemical agriculture mostly because of its expense. We kept needing more and more equipment and then more and more debt to keep up with the equipment. Then I became aware of the dangers—of course, as you are using this stuff, you have to read the labels. Sometimes it seemed to bother you to wear the mask and gloves that were recommended, but I knew our neighbors did not protect themselves.

Then the question occurred to me—is this stuff actually harming farmers? I had no sense at this time that it might be harming the food. Going to chemical fertilizers definitely harmed the soil. It created an impoverishment—a soil without organic matter. That is what started the Dust Bowl.

We ended the devastation of our soil by growing strictly organic matter for several years straight and just plowing it under. Then I made the mistake of bringing us back to chemical agri-culture, harvesting and taking away the organic matter and putting down the chemicals. My Kansas farm was actually rela-tively successful. Our family was making our bank payments. But I saw a lot of farmers that were not successful because they did not do it all as carefully as we did.

So that is my background—to be quite natural, start simple, and make one's own compost to enrich the soil. Back then, I think very few people had any notion that being "organic" could be marketed to others. We just knew that we did not want to go back to chemical fertilizers because they made the soil poor. The pesticides, insecticides, and herbicides were a danger for the farmer and the land.

The first gardening the Resource Center did was in these vacant lots. People who lived on the block, or who hung out in the area would help create compost, clean the sites, and plant. We

called that project "Turn A Lot Around." Pun intended. This was the early 1970s.

Now we have grown, named the project more ambitiously City Farm and have several other sites in the city that sustain a few jobs. But city support is crucial if our program is to grow. Selling the produce pays for maintenance and a salary for the workers, but the start-up costs are big.

The average cost of turning an acre of wasteland into productive farmland is about $20,000. We have suggested to the city that, given the advantages to the municipality of lots being productive and being used for job creation, the city should invest in the initial emptying and enriching the soil. From there on, it can be a self-sustaining farm. The city has initially been positive about City Farm, but they have not committed to new locations at this point. They are looking for a five-acre site, but there are many hurdles.

I think the time has come for Chicago to commit to the idea of urban agriculture on a citywide scale. Chicago has 6000 acres of unused land. 42,000 full-time jobs could be supported by the land if all of it were cultivated. City Farm gives more than food and jobs. It allows people to produce for themselves. Local ownership means that everybody nearby has a stake in the success of a farm. Entire neighborhoods are being transformed.

Our civilization can be so unimaginative. We think that someone else is going to take care of everything. It does not take much to realize that if someone is hanging around making bottles empty, someone else can show them where the glass factory is that wants empty bottles. That is what making a City Farm is about. There are communities where the only commerce and jobs are in the drug trade. What if it were in agricultural production?

The Mobile
City Farmstead

BY THE MOBILE CITY FARMSTEAD TEAM

Our team has partnered with Ken Dunn to provide a design for a mobile storage and office facility for his newest urban farm, called City Farm, located at the corner of Division and Clybourn, next door to the Cabrini-Green housing project. Although we are using the Division and Clybourn farm as our site, the intent is that this facility can be duplicated on other sites as well.

We're calling this facility The Mobile City Farmstead. It will provide tool and produce storage, sheltered workspace, an office, restroom, temporary housing for one employee, and a small farm stand. The Farmstead will also serve to anchor the site, focusing attention to the entry point and providing a place from which to conduct educational classes, tours, and summer-time dinner gatherings.

The architectural components that make up the Farmstead will be those that are salvaged, cheap, degradable and, especially, easily transportable—such as shipping containers, chain-link fencing, canvas, and straw bales. The idea of mobility is critical since City Farm must be able to relocate quickly when the site is sold or ready for redevelopment. While the Farmstead will lend City Farm a sense of establishment (key to the success of any business venture), it will sit as lightly on the land as the agriculture itself.

Together, the agriculture and architecture will give new life to once forgotten pieces of the urban landscape, encouraging curious onlookers to become educated consumers and participants, thereby generating momentum for the drive toward a local, sustainable economy.

The Mobile City Farmstead Team is Matthew Kuhl, Karin Lucas, Dan Rappel, AIA, Amy Struckmeyer, and Shwetha Subramanian.

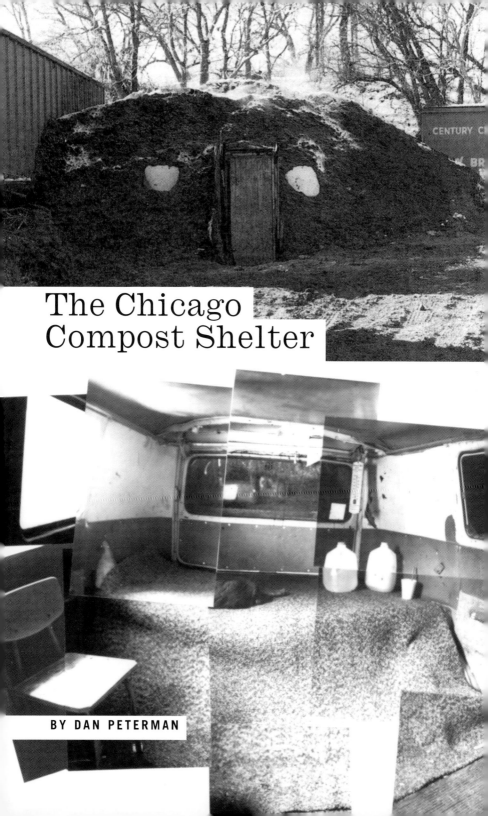

The Chicago
Compost Shelter

BY DAN PETERMAN

The Chicago Compost Shelter is a public installation of experimental architecture. The shelter is designed to stay warm throughout the entire winter by utilizing the heat produced by the decaying process of organic material.

The shelter consists of a Volkswagen van body, which has been buried in a large pile of compost. A small entranceway has been added along with skylights that allow natural light to illuminate the interior. The van itself, with seats removed, is large enough for a bed and some space-conscious furnishings. It comes equipped with ashtrays, a mirror, and armrests. If one cares to hook up a battery, there is a radio and a dome-light.

The compost used for the shelter has been collected as part of a project to recycle organic waste in Chicago by the Resource Center, a non-profit recycling organization. The leaves, grass, clippings, and horse manure will be turned into humus and sold to gardeners and commercial landscapers as a soil conditioner.

A profile of homeless in Chicago done by the Chicago Coalition for the Homeless [in 1988] indicates that about 16% of Chicago's estimated 25,000 homeless generate income through the recycling of cans, glass, and paper. This dependence on recycling by the homeless has revealed itself in recent years through the construction of makeshift shelters in an abandoned lot next to the recycling center. These temporary homes in truck boxes or of scavenged lumber have emerged organically as a response to the compatible work structure which recycling provides.

A mixture of horse manure and wood shavings collected from the Chicago Police stables was used for constructing the Compost Shelter. While decomposing, this material reaches temperatures well in excess of 100 degrees Fahrenheit. It has maintained a temperature of over 75 degrees F inside the shelter through the months of January and February even while temperatures dropped below zero outside. When freshly collected, this mixture of wood shavings and manure emits an ammonia-like smell that disappears quickly after being exposed to fresh air. Visitors to the shelter have experienced no unpleasant odors.

far left top:
Exterior view of the Compost Shelter
Photo, Dan Peterman

far left bottom:
Interior view of the Compost Shelter
Photo collage, Dan Peterman

Mixtures of leaves and grass with the proper moisture content produce similar results.

The Compost Shelter is located on Chicago's South Side at 71st and Dorchester. It is adjacent to a recycling yard run by the Resource Center that attracts a steady stream of customers. Twenty-five to 30 people, traveling by foot, arrive each day throughout the winter. Of these, many appear to live difficult lives on the streets or perhaps squatting in abandoned buildings.

For an example of the organic architecture of events, we have the Resource Center itself. Roads, pathways, piles, and arrangements of materials all develop as needed, in response to a plan that begins arbitrarily and evolves through a cybernetic structure.

The idea of the compost shelter evolved the same way. The buses were there, the compost pile was there, and the use of truck-bodies as winter shelter was already established nearby, as was the danger and difficulty of heating them with available materials. Composting manure generates heat. As the facts shuffle and combine, so do the materials.

With the shelter at its center, we get a sense of the compost pile as a living thing. It has a lifespan that comes to equal the winter for which it is needed. The heat it generates equals, in a sense, life. At the end of the cycle it becomes inert, and dies. This hot/cold cycle reverses the calendar of the seasons, opening up that larger cycle.

The buses at the Center form a sort of social unit of their own. There are perhaps 14 of them, of which about half work at any given time. They are in a constant process of breakdown and recycling of parts; a constant social exchange, forming a sort of social whole in defiance of the obsolescence, entropy, overload, and rust that have doomed them.

Historically these shelters have become victims of city bulldozers. Some have burned as a result of heating with open fires. The Compost Shelter is a continuation of this architectural process, with an emphasis on understanding local social patterns and resources.

Aside from its functional aspects, the Compost Shelter adds an element of irony. The same profile of homelessness goes on to state that, as to interpersonal difficulties, the street people inter-

viewed indicated that the police are one of the top causes of "hassles." The Compost Shelter, heated by manure from police horses creates a fragile network of interdependence between the police and the homeless recyclers. The manure is a city resource being applied to those most in need.

An appropriate accessory for the Compost Shelter would be the installation of a composting toilet for human wastes. A number of designs are available.

The authority of the policeman on horseback contrasts with the position of the collector/squatter. The compost shelter

Mounted police officer, Chicago
Photo, Dan Peterman

proposes a kind of symbiotic relationship between these two, one that is not normally perceived to exist. The shelter proposes itself as an image of the fragile network of interdependency that already and always exists between insiders and outsiders, the center and the margin. The Chicago Mounted Patrol performs mostly duties of crowd control in dense traffic situations. The horseman sits above the crowd as a symbol of order and authority. His horse is both the vehicle of that authority and a generator of useful manure. The policeman surveys the crowd. Within the crowd is the collector who surveys the ground looking for bottles and cans. The policeman is at the center, the collector at the margin. All of these relationships return and are recycled by the Compost Shelter. Center and margin are reversed and thereby disclosed.

This essay originally appeared in WhiteWalls *#19, Spring 1988.*

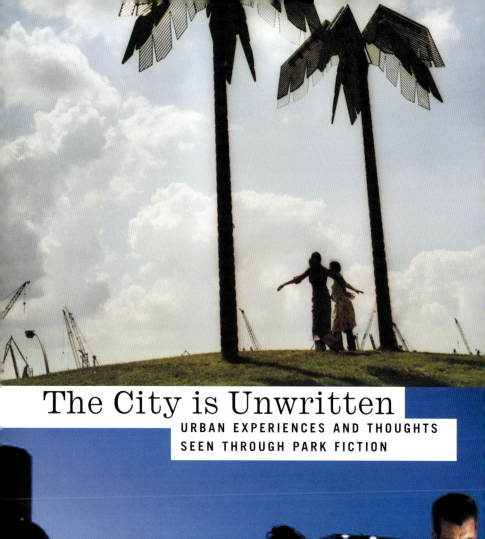

The City is Unwritten

URBAN EXPERIENCES AND THOUGHTS
SEEN THROUGH PARK FICTION

BY CHRISTOPH SCHÄFER

But advisable it is, to confront the mythical powers with trickery and recklessness. —Walter Benjamin

BARRICADE DAYS

The St. Pauli neighborhood of Hamburg is the poorest in Western Germany, though Hamburg, paradoxically, is the second richest city in the European Union. St. Pauli stretches to the Elbe River and is densely built. Public space is rare and what little exists is heavily occupied by tourism, cappuccino addicts, and the red light district. More than 50 percent of the residents have no German passport. So the situation is tense.

Winter '87 began a decisive year for Hamburg and in my life. That winter is now known in local history as the "barricade days" for the assault on the heroic squat on Hafenstrasse in the St. Pauli neighborhood. Barricades erected around the squat to prevent the police from entering the territory surrounded half of this neighborhood. St. Pauli was unified against the government. The Hafenstrasse struggle was breaking news, and fears of a riot if the police rushed to clear the area and demolish the houses were not exaggerated. During the struggle a service was established to guide school kids through the barricades. The best bands in town played nightly on an improvised stage in front of the squatted homes with the help of electricity stolen or supplied by neighbors. In every advertising agency a poster with "Hafenstrasse viel gut!" (Neanderthal-type German for "Harbor Street much good!") was the cool thing to have. The senseless police brutality was too obvious to ignore and moved even some conservative citizens to side with the rebels. I was a person on the fringe supporting, as many did, the clever tactics of the squatters, but far away from the frontline.

After fourteen days the government abandoned their eviction attempt. Eventually the Hafenstrasse squat was legalized. A temporary autonomous zone came into existence before we knew to call it such. A piece of land had been shot out of the map of state control. The struggle inspired Hamburg's left to ini-

far left top:
Palm Tree Island

far left bottom:
Schwabinggrad Ballett performing during Unlikely Encounters in Urban Space congress

tiate projects like Hamburg's free radio station, FSK, still playing hard today. This success left behind a network and a sense of what was possible in the St. Pauli community. The barricade days also marked a turning point. They were the last large-scale confrontational militant action in Hamburg for years to come. The barricade days, in their scale and their shocking consequences were not repeatable. Afterwards, the city government was determined not to let anything like it happen ever again. The government refined their negotiating skills, their repressive instruments were adapted, and they developed more powerful but soft-looking tools of surveillance.

ACID HOUSE

Also in '87, a new method of operating and moving appeared, a change in paradigm that is still unfolding. For me, it started with music from Chicago and Detroit. Acid house music, more than probably any music style before it, is more about mixing—playing pre-recorded tracks—than about live music produced by a live band. While punk rockers questioned the band-audience relation by storming the stage, house was about people dancing, and not about being "the audience" in the first place. Consumers became participants irreversibly. What also started with acid was the conscious idea and ability to create situations. "Raves," the temporary and unauthorized use of empty buildings, became a mass activity.

The disco became a place to celebrate the city by intensifying and transforming that which gets on one's nerves in the daytime. If a city is noisy, polluted, and crowded, a good disco is a joyful place because it is louder, stinking of smoke, perfume and sweat, and too full. Maybe it was the use of psychedelics that gave us the sudden ability to trust one another and see oneself as part of a collective with the power to construct situations, but suddenly, everyday urban life was the most exciting starting point. An adventurous spirit drove us into the strangest of places to produce encounters and surprising events in the most unlikely spaces.

The city was full of possibilities. An aquarium in a Thai restaurant was definitely not a sign of petite bourgeois squareness, as New Left theory would have it, but a miniature garden or a

promise of happiness, a window into imaginary worlds. At the local carnival we no longer saw the automatic photo machines that take your picture during your ride as a sad commercial sign of alienation, but as a sick yet reflexive tool.

This changed point of view, and a newfound ability to redefine spaces, was definitely one of the starting points of Park Fiction. A rave called "Park Fiction in St. Pauli—beatbombs on Berlin" half-ironically renamed all of the little pieces of land left at the harbor wall that would become part of Park Fiction according to their everyday use. The space between the squatted houses roamed by a gang of rotten punk-dogs was renamed "Hafentreppenhunderpark" (Harbor Staircase Dog Park). A slope usually occupied by heavy drinkers was renamed "Bierdosenpark" (Beer Can Park). These "parks" were transformed into different "areas" for that rave, and the name of the Park Fiction project was born.

PRIVATIZED VIEW—SOCIALIZED SHADOW

Hamburg is now marketing itself as the New Media Harbor City. For this reason the dominant ideology in current Hamburg city politics is image-policy meant to cultivate this identity. Park Fiction began in 1995 at the same time as the harbor wall along the Elbe River was being sold off to new media companies. The city government planned to obstruct St. Pauli's last view of the river with a block of heavy buildings along the harbor wall. The neighborhood did not want these buildings. We wanted a public park instead. But authorities always ignore desires like this. Because the Elbe shoreline—the harbor wall—is a place where power particularly likes to represent itself, our desires were even more hopeless. Things that might be tolerated in other places as interesting alternative flavors are automatically confronting power and the dominant ideology in this location. For both sides every step taken on this undeveloped green space is symbolic.

Demands for the park rather than the harbor wall development were carried out by a network left over from the Hafenstrasse struggles, especially social workers from the local community center, GWA (Community Center of St. Pauli-South), priests, and the visionary headmistress of a local school.

They managed to arrange negotiations with the local politicians. Lingering behind these negotiations was the threat that a militant struggle might light up again. The city needed to avoid this. However, the classic forms of lobbying were about to lead to a dead end. A year after I joined the negotiating group we developed a new set of practices and concepts informed by re-readings of classic Situationist texts and the writings of Henri

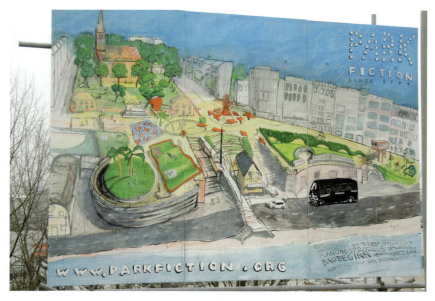

Billboard showing community-led design for the park

Lefebvre, as well as reflections on democratic art projects from the seventies, conceptual art, unsatisfactory public art, and acid-related experiences. This mix precipitated the transfer from "demanding a park" to "Park Fiction." In 1994, the Zapatistas proclaimed, "We decided to stop preaching to people and started to listen." This sentence marked a dramatic rupture in revolutionary thinking and practice, and was a critical model for how we would proceed.

At this point, Park Fiction consisted of myself, Cathy Skenea, and a local network of St Pauli neighbors, social institutions, the nearby church, squatters, artists, shop and café owners, together with the intense Hamburg music scene based around the Golden Pudel Klub (Golden Poodles Club), a club located in a tiny old house right in our park, which the government would have liked to demolish too. The Golden Pudel

was founded by Schorsch Kamerun and Rocko Schamoni, musicians from a scene around Die Goldenen Zitronen (The Golden Lemon) a band that began in the eighties as fun punks, played during the Hafenstrasse riots, turned down offers by major labels, and developed a place for poetry, artists, and experimental bands. The impact of Park Fiction's connection with the Golden Pudel cannot be overestimated. The club opened a field of resonance with musical subcultures, which often feature higher style awareness and playful relationships with social codes so often missing in political groups and their reliance on objective analysis of conditions. Of course, bands also attract a lot of people.

PRODUCTION OF DESIRES

We had to find different ways to operate if we wanted to engage public space as a field of dispute. Political groups on the left, as well as the rulers on the right, usually underestimate art; none of them take it seriously. As sad as this is at times, it can also be beneficial to those making art because many of your actions will escape suspicion. With this in mind, Park Fiction started collectively producing desires: lectures and park-related exhibitions in the local church, shop windows, in schools and so on. We worked to open a little "parallel knowledge universe."

On the streets and the slope of land for which we were fighting we staged *Activities Anticipating the Park.* We had an open-air cinema, agit-prop slide shows, and raves. Shortly after Park Fiction's actions began, Cathy Skenea and I were invited by the state cultural board, who were unaware of Park Fiction at that time, to develop a plan for a public artwork. We did not want to plop down a sculpture, instead we suggested developing Park Fiction. A park by the harbor wall was already a real thing on many levels—in the community's mind, in the hip and trendy music scene, and on the national art scene. So we approached the state with demands.

Park Fiction's initial idea was to organize a parallel planning process and a collective production of desires for the park without being commissioned to do so by authorities. We developed a process that was open and approachable by anyone who

wished to take part in planning for a real place connecting arts and social movements without falling into the trap of taking the "legal" bureaucratic path. This planning process was supplemented by a program we called *Infotainment*, which included lectures on parks and politics, parks and their ideological backgrounds, and what filmmaker Margit Czenki called "art and politics making each other more clever."

When the politicians finally entered the scene they found themselves in a complex field where they had difficultly moving. For a short moment in time we made the rules of the game. We had a lively idea of what we were doing and firm ground under our feet. They were in the "stupid" position, looking like what they are, boring people who just block things, which they did. The cultural board agreed to finance Park Fiction in early '96, but the senator for urban development cancelled our funding later that same year when he heard about our project. So that winter we made the decision to take more militant action to pressure the authorities. Things, however, developed differently.

HARBOR HOSPITAL

The city decided to demolish the very popular Harbor Hospital in St. Pauli. The hospital is only half a mile away from the park. After clearing the first wing of the hospital, to the government's surprise, the empty building was squatted by activists. The squatters were strongly supported by the neighborhood. Weekly demonstrations took place, and for the first time ever

The Park Fiction archive at Documenta 11, Kassel Germany, 2002

there was a strike in the red light district. 1997 was an election year making the government ready to negotiate on the hospital and any other problems in St. Pauli to calm the movement. A round table dealing with the park was installed; those of us from the neighborhood were on one side, the authorities on the other.

Round tables are dangerous things; their name suggests an equal balance of power while the shape conceals the unequal status of the participants. Speaking with bureaucrats means half-accepting their—the dominant—way of thinking and negotiating. In this case it was unavoidable, but we managed to agree that Park Fiction would occupy the space along the harbor wall, and Park Fiction would organize the planning process. As a sign of trust, we demanded that the budget for the project, blocked by the senator for urban development, be transferred to our bank account before the elections. This happened and we began.

DEVICES

We organized a project, *The Planning Process Like a Game,* giving out game-boards instead of leaflets that described the access points where one could become involved in our process. We opened a planning container that held the *Modeling Clay Office,* a telephone hotline for people who were inspired late at night, a garden library, and a project called the *Archive of Desires.* There was also the *Action Kit*—a mobile planning office with questionnaires, maps, dough, dictaphone, foldout harbor panorama, and instamatic camera to capture ideas.

We employed pseudo-sociological instruments, quoting and recycling tactics from a deeply social-democratic era in the late '60s and early '70s, while referring to the betrayed promises of the past. The difference between our methods and that of most social workers is in our work concept—integrating artists, designers, programmers, researchers, and shop owners, in a non-hierarchical rhizomatic open process. We believed that our planning process had to allow artistic practice the potential for autonomy, resistance, and unwieldiness. Collaborating with others should not mean reducing yourself to a social worker. Nor should it mean reducing your artistic work to the administration of the creativity of others.

We were not objective. We took sides from the beginning. Using our skills we played with the forms that power, corporate culture, and mainstream media use to denigrate small projects relative to their existing wealth. For example, we fashioned a planning container painted the same colors as the Info Box used at the Potsdamer Platz construction site in Berlin, the biggest corporate building site ever in Germany. As a tonic for the exclu-

The planning container

sion of the citizens and the parliament from the planning process, the developers of the Potsdamer Platz constructed the Info Box. The box was filled with three-dimensional animations of the archi-tecture, sculpted heads of the architects, and all kinds of "participatory" games like a chessboard that featured chess figures shaped in the style of the buildings. Our planning container, by contrast, was filled with materials exploring what a city could be, and offered many possibilities for the visitor to directly influence our planning process.

In 1998, we determined the riverfront park's focus in two community conferences. The park would consist of "islands" with different functions, designed by different people. Together as a group we chose only the general functions of the park and picked favorite designs. We did not want the ideas to become

neutralized by consensus, so after the initial decision the individual or group behind each design was allowed to complete their designs according to their own vision. Through this approach, Park Fiction claimed a public space for the non-commercial production of the neighborhood's desires.

WHOOWNSTHECITY

In 2001, an investor bought the Kasematten, a building underneath a part of the Park Fiction area. The investor immediately made himself known in the community by chopping down trees in front of the houses along the Hafenstrasse. A month later sections of the park and the Kasematten were suddenly surrounded by fences guarded by security men. Shortly thereafter, a glass-aluminum construction was erected in front of the Kasematten for a special event, called Media Night, paid for by the government to accompany the national New Media Congress "Hamburger Dialog."

At this time very few members were active with Park Fiction. The headmistress had left the school and the priests were busy with other concerns. Those of us left protested the use of Park Fiction territory by the investor and scrutinized the situation in a flyer called *That's Gentrification*.

Because of our publication support came from sides we did not expect. First from electro-musicians associated with the Pudel Klub who understood the investor's presence as a threat to the last remaining free and cheap spaces left in Hamburg, and who were especially angry at the DJ's who agreed to spin at Media Night. Support also came from Rote Flora, a squatted autonomous cultural center in the north of St. Pauli, whose building was sold by the city to the same investor. And, late but crucial support came from former squatters in Hafenstrasse.

After our flyer, someone created a witty counterfeit letter that really kicked things off. In it, the City Development Company (STEG) invited everybody in the neighborhood for a glass of champagne and a chance to mingle with new media people during Media Night. Of course STEG publicly denied having written that invitation, and this denial appeared in all the newspapers.

Then, a day before the Media Night, Schorsch and Rocko from the Pudel Klub declared themselves "official supporters" of the event, dressed as investors in white construction helmets, and shot a fast video about the numerous corporate buildings rising along the river, dropping all the catchphrases of neo-liberal newspeak: win-win-situation, subcultural ambience, private-public partnership, etcetera. Our group planned an information stand and an open-air screening of Margit Czenki's movie *Park Fiction—desire will leave home and take to the streets*.

By the afternoon of the event hundreds of police had blocked the entire area around the Kasematten. Residents were barred from their houses. People who started to protest were beaten. Protesters threw money at the politicians and investors, shocking the new media people arriving at the party. Schorsch and Rocko's video was shown on a giant screen outside Pudel Club, with the Park Fiction film screened on the other side, projected over the heads of the police lines from a neighboring house.

After the events many of the participants formed a short-lived but effective group called *wemgehoertdiestadt* (*whoownsthecity*) that organized a well-received press conference analyzing the protest and the function of subcultures in rundown areas before they are gentrified. Later wemgehoertdiestadt organized an event for re-appropriation of the Kasematten. The bad press caused the investor to never hold another event in this location. But still, in spring 2004, the Park Fiction area of the Kasematten is fenced in.

FLYING CARPET

After nine years of activity, the park is finally being realized. Two components officially opened in September 2003: the *Palm Tree Island or Tea Garden*, and the *Flying Carpet*. Summer 2003 was the hottest in history and people used the park heavily in a variety of nice unplanned manners. For instance, whenever the sun was shining at five in the afternoon, some fifteen to thirty three-year-olds entered the park to play on the flying carpet. This was an age group we did not consider at all because you would not have seen them in the public spaces of St. Pauli before the park existed.

Nine years is, however, too long for such a small project. During the long process and the close negotiations with author-

ities in the realization phase, key parts of the project have been damaged, forgotten, or corrupted. Some significant parts of the design may not be realized at all. For example, the *Pirate Fountain*, featuring translucent images of Anne Bonny and Mary Read, two cruel eighteenth-century Caribbean pirate leaders that would glow blood red and poison green at night, is not financed, and one of the most popular designs, the *Strawberry-shaped Treehouse*, has fallen from the plan completely.

For us, it is not certain at this time if we can continue cooperating with the authorities. We can do so only if central elements are built, and if our vision for a link between the urban everyday and the imaginary is visible in the design of the park. If, instead the integrity of the project is corrupted and designs are boiled down to the uninspired urban planning you see on every corner, we will cancel our cooperation with a bang.

The Flying Carpet, Elbe River, and the Hamburg harbor
Photo, Brett Bloom

UNLIKELY ENCOUNTERS

Independent from these actions we found it necessary to expand our horizons. As a first step, we organized an international congress in 2003, "Park Fiction presents: Unlikely Encounters in Urban Space," as the basis for a possible Institute for Independent Urbanism. We invited groups who, like Park Fiction, attempt to redefine artistic practice under post-industrial conditions. Groups like Sarai Media Lab from Delhi, India; Borderhack

and Maclovio Rojas from Tijuana, Mexico; Ala Plastica from La Plata, Argentina; Cantieri Isola from Milan, Italy; and Ligna and Schwabinggrad Ballett, both also based in Hamburg. The congress events were held at locations throughout St. Pauli, including a disco on Hafenstrasse, the church, the Buttclub, the Harbor City, and on a boat on the river. In conjunction with the congress Park Fiction exhibited a version of the Park Fiction archive, an installation we originally created for Documenta 11 (an international exhibition of contemporary art that occurs every five years in Kassel, Germany). The archive, which features a wide historical collection of posters, drawings, photographs and all form of ephemera, was presented between translucent sails on the Repperbahn, a famous street in St. Pauli. We also organized guides from the community who offered tours through the exhibition and the park.

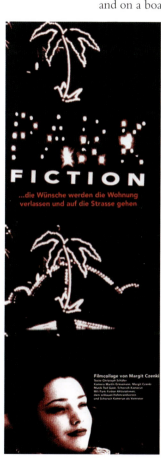

Poster for Margit Czenki's film *Park Fiction—desire will leave home and take to the streets*

With the proposed Institute for Independent Urbanism we will push urban discourse forward. For urbanity, as a discourse, is its own line of thinking and cannot be reduced to "urban planning." We see the urban not as a unified artistic vision, but as a set of practices opposed to the state and not identical with the democratic. The urban is an accumulation of differences where the unexpected can linger. Simply put, a city worth living in is a place of contradictions living with each other, piled up and potentially growing exponentially.

The Institute for Independent Urbansim will build on some of the lessons learned with Park Fiction. We will develop tools, attitudes, courage, practices, and programs that ignore cultural and class borders to make unlikely encounters, meetings, and connections plentiful. The institute will explore constituent practices that avoid addressing the state directly, in favor of street-level investigations for connecting arts and social movements, engaging in alternative forms of science, squatting land, and otherwise challenging dominant systems of urban planning.

MEGACITIES

We were often told that Park Fiction was only possible, only "real," because everybody in the group lived in that specific community, and that the project is not reproducible. But the real reason it is not reproducible is because local situations change too fast, and different groups must develop their own devices and rhythms. I do not believe, however, that in order to work with a place you must be local. Cities are built by the imaginings of the outsiders, the migrants, and the travelers who conceptualize what a particular place could be.

When I visit Mexico City, I see a city where the vast majority of houses were constructed without architects and urban planners. The same is true with Delhi, Jakarta, Calcutta, Dhaka, and Buenos Aires. In contrast to these informal cities, Northern European cities look like three-dimensional realizations of ideologies. Park Fiction has challenged this reduced view of the urban. We have worked so that "public space" can produce desires, relate the city to the imaginary, and be rooted in the urban everyday.

Today, it doesn't seem farfetched to believe that the financial crisis of Argentina could happen in the major centers of global capital sooner or later. From this view, small art projects, informal encounters in a park, or innocent acidic experiences like mine constitute letters sent from the about-to-vanish-past to a very near future where we will have to reinvent cities and our everyday lives on a much bigger scale. In Hamburg-St. Pauli, our aim was to stop the city government from blocking our last existing public view of the harbor. At first glance this project might look exactly like the opposite of struggles around informal settlements in the cities of the Global South where neighborhoods are often demolished by the government to be replaced with public parks. But to us the informal settlements, like our park, are the blueprint for possible cities of the future. Cities that ignore the architectural trade. Cities that are a product of the people who inhabit them, not the business of specialist urban planners. Cities that exist as a deep and genuine rupture.

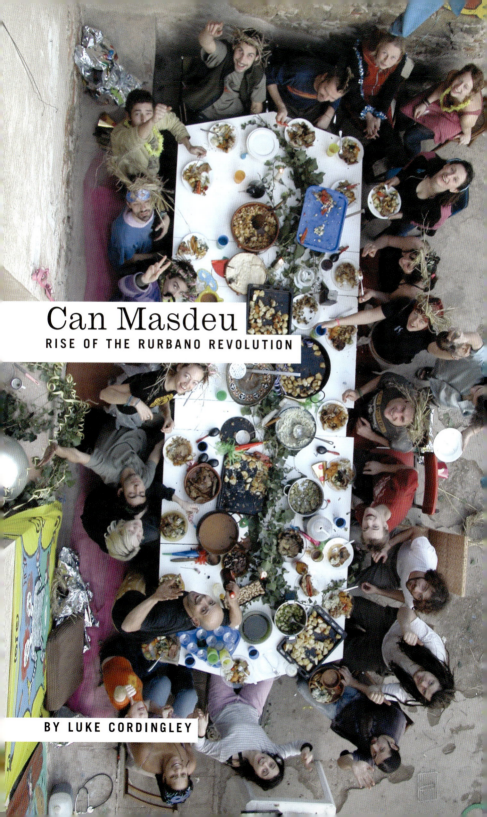

Can Masdeu

RISE OF THE RURBANO REVOLUTION

BY LUKE CORDINGLEY

Barcelona, Spain, sprawls down to the waters of the Mediterranean from the pine forested mountains of the Collserolla National Park, a swath of rich, ecologically diverse green terrain that until now has stood as a timeless divide between Barcelona and surrounding towns and cities on the other side of the mountains. From the high vantage point of the Collserolla, Barcelona appears as if it is being operated on, the skyline dotted with hundreds of tall cranes, robots surgically dismantling and reconstructing the city in a perpetual cycle of speculation, displacement, and gentrification. The city continues to be a magnet for economic immigration, both national and international. Walking in the narrow streets of the old town it is impossible not to bear witness to the massive changes the city continues to undergo. One can hear as much Arabic as Catalan, as much English as Castilian. And as the center is gentrified, and the suburbs fill, the city penetrates the Collserolla, leaving deep and permanent scars in the beautiful rolling hillsides of the park.

A political tourist to Barcelona will find a myriad of diverse grassroots struggles. Virtually nothing is left uncovered by the vast, integrated and highly organized, yet chaotically Mediterranean social movements. On December 22, 2001, a drop was cast into this ocean. An internationally-mixed group occupied an abandoned building and its grounds called Can Masdeu. Located in the Valley of Saint Genis, where the green seas of the Collserolla National Park collide with the concrete jungle of Barcelona, the community of Can Masdeu was born.

THE RISING TIDE

Can Masdeu is a huge mansion on ample grounds. Records date the house and grounds back to Roman times. One can presume the site was chosen for settlement for its ability to harness surface run-off water and nature's subterranean aquatic systems. At the house you have the impression you are in the forested countryside. South facing terraced hillsides and medieval water systems fit harmoniously into the natural character of the

far left: Christmas dinner at Can Masdeu

The Can Masdeu mansion
surrounded by gardens

surrounding mountains and valley. The lush grounds of Can
Masdeu form a valley within a valley. A ten-minute walk down
the track, however, leaves you at the frontline of Barcelona's
urban sprawl. Twenty-five minutes on bike brings you to the city
center. Can Masdeu, rather than being in the forest, is set in a
barrio (neighborhood) community.

The immediate aim of our occupation was to secure a venue
in which to host the international conference of the Rising Tide
for Climate Justice Campaign due to take place in February of
2002. Three hundred activists—largely European, but also including representatives from Soweto, Morocco, Nepal, and West
Papua—were coming to attend. Detritus was cleared, glass recycled, and windows repaired. Sleeping space for all three hundred
participants was prepared. Main electricity was located nearby
and a basic rewire of the property undertaken. A few wood
burning stoves were installed, walls knocked out, composting
toilets built, and barricades constructed.

Although most of our early work was focused on the structure of the house, we were already dreaming and conspiring
about the potential of the space. Dedicated work and a sense of
collectivism, community, and anarcho-fluidity were not the only
cornerstones of the project. The search for a water source, and
means to store water from winter into the summer were, already
in this first month, becoming an obsession.

The search for water initiated our relationship with the bio-
diversity of the natural valley. It was also, for this group of

squatting city kids, the first step in the journey to recover knowledge lost from the radar of modern society, to learn from it, add to it, and bring it back into the public domain. To us urbanites accustomed to turning a tap for unlimited drinking water and to flushing liters of this precious material down the toilet, the daily two kilometer round trip to collect water from the city with a heavy cart was more than a simple shock to the system. We experienced the hardship and pressures of life without a stable and local fresh water supply. Suddenly, the countless images we had all seen of African women journeying for hours everyday to collect water became real. We felt the weight of water, the physical exertion, the endurance, and the motivation required by countless people the world over, simply to bring this fundamental human right from the source to the cooking pot. That month taught us what remains the most fundamental lesson we have learned. Water is life.

BETWEEN ARCHAEOLOGY AND INNOVATION

Evidence of an ancient dilapidated irrigation system was all over the land and the building was full of tubes and pipes, even a broken toilet. So where had the water come from? Without knowing the water lines, and with the property owners barring our access to the survey plans, our options were limited. We turned to the elders of the neighboring community. The need to answer the water question gave birth to this most beautiful aspect of the Can Masdeu community, the symbiotic relationship between young and old people in the barrio. This created a constant two-way exchange of information between generations, realities, and mindsets.

People in the barrio have witnessed the abandoned, closed off, and neglected house and gardens of Can Masdeu deteriorate for the last fifty years. Some remembered the building in its final days as a leper hospital. They felt the injustice as the landowners criminally left the beautiful architecture and cultivation to degrade while the value of the land continued to increase in a flagrant example of property speculation.

This popular sense of disgust with the landowners quickly enabled us to build strong relations within the barrio. Combining

their knowledge with our enthusiasm, we set out to unearth the water system, striving to understand both its complexities and its beautiful simplicities. The dilapidated water system is a gravity fed system that harvests rainwater into a series of open tanks, a huge tank on a hill behind the house, and smaller tanks spread throughout the terraces. The tanks are connected by a complex series of open brick channels, which weave an intricate path down the steps and along the terraces to provide irrigation for cultivation of the land.

This style of gravity fed water system was brought to Catalonia by Moorish conquerors in the seventh century and the system at Can Masdeu appears to have been constructed at the very beginning of the sixteenth century. The drinking water for the house comes from a different branch of the same system, a series of water mines, which are narrow and low brick tunnels, some up to three hundred meters long are dug deep into the hills. These mines intercept underground aquifers. The aquifers were in disrepair when we arrived, and unfortunately the channels to the house still have not been found.

A great aspect of squatting old buildings is the mixture of archaeology and innovation needed to make a space usable. Somewhere between low tech and no tech is squat tech. Squat tech is assessing available resources, appreciating that most of them are broken or in disrepair, and dismantling existing items in order to use their parts for more urgent functions. In this case, through an interesting process of old community knowledge, archaeology, and squat tech innovation, we managed to get one of the water mines to feed into a spring in the gardens near the house just in time for the Rising Tide Campaign. In just over a month, the small group of okupas (occupiers/squatters) transformed a derelict space, abandoned for over 50 years, into a rudimentary but functioning social center.

By the end of the conference, our core group had increased in size from twelve to twenty four, and our vision was clear. The activists that participated in the Rising Tide conferences, combined with the fact we had not been evicted, fueled ideas for the life and project we wanted to create. We would create an urban social center based on rural principles: a rurbano social center. At

Can Masdeu we could have our cake and eat it too. We were tied to the land, while in the midst of urban political networks. Here we would reverse the invasion of the city on the country by renovating the house, clearing and cultivating a small garden, and learning to live within the finite balances of the valley. Then the eviction notice arrived.

Women trying to break police lines with water for the climbers

RESISTING EVICTION

The Can Masdeu project was off to a successful start. At a time when we were distracted by the European Union summit bringing European heads of state to Barcelona, the property owners of Can Masdeu decided to move against us okupas. The hospital trust fund—the owners of the property—whose three board members are the city government, the regional government, and the Catholic Church, sought and won an eviction order set for late May 2002. Our group chose to resist non-violently, but with active confrontation.

In the weeks leading up to the eviction, we kept busy. Drawing on the group's varied experiences of evictions and direct action protest, we relied on strategies harkening back to the road protest tree camps used in the United Kingdom and anti-logging blockades. Attached to the exterior of the house were bathtubs, chairs, and death planks; on the roof there was a tripod and lightning conductor that people could climb and hang from. When the

police arrived at dawn one morning in early June we were ready. At the call: "the police are at the bottom of the track," our defense machine went into action. Nobody stayed "in the house," as our counter-positions had been constructed outside of the house.

Our resistance surprised the police. These tactics were new in Catalonia and the police had no resources to remove the "climber" okupas. In the meantime some protesters left the grounds to contact the press and supporters in the city. People arrived from the barrio. At the end of the day the police had not made a move, and the evening TV news broadcasted the resistance. People were hanging from the building in the rain, and over a hundred more people were setting up camp in the gardens below. The police never gained control of the situation.

During the first night there were cat and mouse games between the police and the climbers, who were ill equipped to survive a sustained protest, and needed to sneak into the house to recover blankets and nourishment. The following morning the media machine was in overdrive. As with all great media spectacles, the coverage helped create the event. The more the media discussed the resistance, the more people came to join. On the second day there were enough people to march down the hill and block the motorway in protest.

below and far right:
Climbers during
the eviction

At the end of day two, the resistance spread to the city with protesters visiting members of the hospital trust fund. At this time there were over three hundred people camped in the rain. The story was headline news. The police, apart from trying to start a few fights, could only block food and supplies from reaching the climbers.

At dawn on the third day one could see, through the mist of clouds and campfires, a valley full of police vans and press vehi-

cles. We didn't know how long the climbers could sustain resolve without food, water, or sleep. Some, in fact, had already come down. We hired a lawyer who appealed to the judge arguing that the police were acting illegally and inhumanely, unquestionably endangering lives by actively prohibiting food and drink from reaching the climbers. The police responded that this was the quickest method of resolution. With medieval siege tactics they would starve the okupas out.

The judge, in an unprecedented decision, ruled in our favor and called a halt to the eviction. Before word had filtered out to the crowds camped in the gardens and those hanging from the building, the police withdrew. The media went crazy and the regional fame of the Can Masdeu project was established. Nobody knew what to expect for the future, but for now the project survived.

Of course, not everything went perfectly because despite the fact that our eviction story was turned into a children's book, fairy-

tales do not exist. Even as the climbers descended, the first murmurings of discontent could be heard. Some members of the Can Masdeu community simply could not carry on. The rapid dynamic pace had begun that December and went off the dial during the eviction, emotionally and physically destroying some. Others of our group and supporters felt it wrong that we actively engaged the media, which some perceive as a branch of the state propaganda machine. Others claimed we were separating ourselves from the rest of the squatting community, colluding with the press to present the case of "good squatters verses bad squatters," and that the spectacle of our non-violent resistance was overshadowing other struggles.

A press conference that happened spontaneously minutes after the police left

The accusations hurt. In a way they were a continuation of the constant activist debate about violence and non-violence. For many of us veterans of the anti-globalization circuit, this internal conflict had become old and tired. Many of us had actively worked to prove that fundamental differences in tactics could be a source of strength rather than division.

Some of our critics to this day have not been placated. Perhaps this is because we never changed our media strategy. But as long as we do not compromise individuals, projects, or strategies with which we have solidarity, it is sensible to fight and protect our project and ideals with all available strategies, tactics, and tools. It is undeniable that the Can Masdeu project has absorbed a lot of media coverage, but it is debatable whether that means we are drawing attention away from other issues.

FROM EVALUATION TO INITIATION

The early days after the eviction siege saw us living in a continued state of high alert. And the two years following the first eviction attempt have seen a marked increase in political repression both at a local and international level. Many of the oldest occupied social centers in Barcelona have been evicted or are due for eviction, in the culmination of the latest cycle of the property speculation game. In an attempt to rebuild a healthy dialogue with our critics we reinitiated the defunct Okupas Assembly, a monthly meeting open to all the squats in the city, to strengthen existing networks between occupied social centers in Barcelona. The assembly has been crucial for pooling resources, discussing differences in tactics, and collectivizing resistance to threats against our spaces.

The heavy evaluation and decision-making process that followed the eviction fight was too much for some who sadly left Can Masdeu. The remaining group of 20 grasped our potential and reaffirmed a key aim of the group living at Can Masdeu: dedication to permaculture and self-determination while bringing the issues of autonomy and ecology into the political agenda. We continued to rely on a non-hierarchical, consensus-based organization model. There are no votes in meetings, instead decisions are arrived at through a process of discussions, proposals,

Toothbrushes in a shared bathroom

amendments, facilitations, and evaluations that ideally are representative of everyone's opinions. We have a general assembly once every two weeks, a legal assembly once a week, and task-based groups that organize their own commission assemblies when they need to, reporting back to the general meeting for final approval. Life at Can Masdeu sometimes feels like a never-ending string of meetings, conducted after dark so that one can fit two day's work into one.

After seven months of activities we felt we still were not engaging the local community in a permanent enough manner. While the land and house were theoretically open spaces, we were not mounting the educational programs we desired, and had not developed the space into a genuinely open-use entity. Work began again.

The first issue, as always, was the legality of our inhabitation. The path to achieving continued defense for the space was evident: community support. With this type of support we can consistently beat criminal charges by arguing our social legitimacy. For example, when the second eviction notice arrived over three hundred of our neighbors requested that charges also be brought against them, as they too used the space, and therefore were okupas.

We received a lot of help and advice from people who passed through the house on a daily basis. Some planted their own gardens alongside ours, and we struggled to convey to them our message of ecology and autonomy. That November saw the inauguration of the community gardens at Can Masdeu.

BECAUSE GARDENERS ARE WARRIORS

After cleaning one water tank, excavating and restoring another, we had enough irrigation to open up more of the land for cultivation. We posted notices around the barrio advertising that anyone was welcome to some land, provided they were interested in cultivating organic, non-transgenic food, and were prepared to embark on a journey of collective work, learning, and skill sharing. Most people in the Spanish state live in flats with no land. The initial response was enormous and there has been a waiting list for gardens ever since.

Gardeners at Can Masdeu

Today there are over thirty parcels of land worked by over eighty people. The group has organized itself into commissions, some responsible for collective work such as continuing renovation and improvement of the water system. Other commissions are responsible for research into new techniques of water efficient cultivation, plant varieties, etcetera. Others research new and old techniques of permaculture and organic gardening, such as companion planting to naturally discourage pests and disease.

In accordance with our low impact ethics we have developed and evolved many energy efficient systems for the house such as solar water heaters, bike powered sound systems and washing machines, a small solar electricity system, different grey water systems, and composting experiments. We use the compost generated by our dry toilets to cultivate a small orchard of fruit trees. To strive for autonomy we continue to recycle as many of the materials we use as possible.

The community garden project has become one of the key public focuses of the house. The gardens and terraces are the combined domain of the living group and the community gardens group. The neighbors are no longer participating in our project rather we participate in theirs. This has inspired and empowered everyone. We are no longer twenty people protesting eviction, but a hundred and twenty. This influx has enabled us to focus on a myriad of other projects.

THE CLASS OF CAN MASDEU

The hospital trust fund, still the landowner, continues to try to evict us. To this end they advance vague plans for the development of the valley. Before our occupation the land was simply held in speculation of rising value for future profit. But despite the coming infrastructure of two new metro stations nearby and a huge motorway exit at the foot of the hill, the hospital trust can no longer publicly justify its desire to sell the land for demolition and development. Demolition is undoubtedly Can Masdeu's eventual fate should we leave.

Participants in an environmental workshop

To counter us, the hospital trust has presented media savvy plans that are basically legal co-optations of the work we do at Can Masdeu. They propose to use the house and grounds as a "gateway to the Collserolla National Park," setting up an info-point in the house. Given that we have been doing this since our beginning, we decided to evolve our project and open a visitors' center ourselves. We call our center the Punto de Interacion de la Collserolla (PIC).

The PIC is basically a renaming of the largest space in the house at Can Masdeu to serve our legal and media strategies. In the PIC there is a library, research station, info-stall, free shop, an exhibition about the Collserolla's flora and fauna, maps of good bike

rides and the zones endangered by urbanization. It is a space many groups use for meetings, presentations, and events. The living community also uses it to mount some of its own projects and initiatives. Groups of school children taking part in our environmental education program begin the day in the PIC, later moving to the gardens then into the valley. This room is used every Sunday to mount our School Without Teachers, a series of workshops and activities aimed to deliver information about and techniques for existing autonomously. These workshops are public, free, and extremely diverse. The program between January and May 2004 featured workshops on Chinese herbal medicine, wild medicinal plants of the Collserolla, edible plants and mushrooms, the political and ecological situation in Venezuela, how to make shoes, and how to deal with trauma resulting from police repression.

We continue to organize actions and campaigns in Barcelona while also participating as an affinity group in annual anti-globalization mobilizations. After hosting a training weekend for the Street Medics Network, an affinity group from our house left for the 2003 protests against the G8 Summit in Evian, France, though the group never actually took to the streets as medics.

One morning when the heads of state were due to meet, our group deployed as a non-violent blockade to prohibit translators from reaching the conference center, attempting to paralyze this conference of the illegitimate and unaccountable. Two climbers dangled from either side of a single rope that blocked the Aubonne roadway on a bridge over a shallow river. The police cut the rope despite warnings that there were people on both ends. One of the climbers fell over twenty meters sustaining severe injuries; the other was saved by the quick reactions of activists on the bridge who caught her rope.

This repressive violence was a defining moment for many of us. Some of us flew to Switzerland to care for the climbers, to deal with the press and legal work, and to bond with other anti-repression groups. Others back in Barcelona joined international solidarity actions, occupying first the French, and later the Swiss embassies. Another group from our house hung from the seventh floor Swiss embassy for a week to maintain international press coverage on this brutal police violence.

The Aubonne roadway incident left us to reflect that as a group we did not allow time to deal with some of our most fundamental and deep-set psychological, emotional, and gender issues. The short-term reactionary dynamics of urban activism, together with the stress of living in a house with twenty-five or more people, fostered many inter-personal issues we were not adequately addressing. Together we reprioritized, wanting better ways to care for our emotions and weaknesses at a communal level. Assemblies for emotional growth became more frequent. Today, with most of the building work complete, our main internal focus is our personal and collective well-being. In summer 2004 we organized, an encounter in Geneva, Switzerland focusing on the emotional ramifications of repression.

Despite the pull outward, at the end of 2003 we decided to limit our external political activity, not at the personal level, but as an organized group. From that point forward the community would only work on anti-land-speculation campaigns, anti-repression campaigns, and agro-ecological issues. Although the list contains three headings, each campaign contains its own list of sub-sections. For example, agro-ecology includes such diverse yet connected issues as gene technology, agro-autonomy, the flooding of the Itoiz valley in Northern Spain, and natural medicinal autonomy. The anti-repression campaign not only includes highlighting and fighting the rising number of incidents of violent repression in mainland Europe, but also forging a model for social movements to be better prepared in dealing with the emotional trauma caused by repression. We have refined our approach so that any external campaign we involve ourselves in maintains a direct connection with the evolution of our life as a living group, the heart of the Can Masdeu project.

Of course, in this article there is not enough space to touch upon the diversity of the hundreds who participate in Can Masdeu and its satellite projects. Today Can Masdeu facilities include: a ceramic workshop and kiln—the clay harvested from hillsides in the valley, a wood-fired bread oven built and fuelled by resources available in the valley, the PIC, a sauna, solar powered systems, the community gardens, grey water systems, a yoga room, a bike repair workshop, a forge, direct action and

climbing training, a flamenco studio, another dance studio, a cinema, and a party room. We host a hack lab, run youth education, use our bike powered sound system at city demonstrations and barrio carnivals, host meetings of—and sit on—various grassroots platforms. We also cultivate a variety of gardens, including a medicinal herb garden, an edible garden, and show gardens all with organic methods. We replant the valley with indigenous species while felling and harvesting non-indigenous species for construction and fuel. Raised chickens provide a constant source of food for neighboring wild animals, and the occasional egg for the kitchen.

Fraggle Band

THE FUTURE IS WAITING

2004 is the second anniversary of continued resistance at Can Masdeu. The pace of life remains as fast as ever as we continue to balance the contradictory dynamics of a squatted, and therefore temporary, project working with issues of permaculture and sustainability. The okupas of Can Masdeu are entering into the final stages of an un-winnable legal battle. Our concepts and the hospital trust fund's concepts are contradictory. We are combating individualism with collectivism and dependence with autonomy, but no one knows for sure what the future

holds. One thing is for certain, the valley of Can Masdeu will never be the same again.

Even the worst-case scenario is not so bad. An eviction of Can Masdeu will leave it stronger than ever. After two planes destroyed the twin towers, the absence of those universally known symbols became more symbolic than their prior presence. The eviction and destruction of a successfully created autonomous collective strengthens the ideals our collective fights for. Complete autonomy is the aim. After all, in the wider human and planetary context, Can Masdeu, and the sustainable, anti-capitalist ideal it stands for is inevitable. And if somehow we stay, well, who knows?

Stay or go, we are only as legitimate and autonomous as we perceive ourselves to be. This is a fundamental of anarchy, and in Can Masdeu exists anarchy so pure, so fluid and so strong, that some cannot even see it.